I0044794

# Sports Law Handbook
# (For Coaches and Administrators)

## William H. Glover, Jr., J.D.

# SPORTS LAW HANDBOOK

## (For Coaches and Sports Administrators)

*Copyright © 2009 by Author: William H. Glover Jr. J.D.*

*All rights reserved. Except as permitted under the US Copyright Act 1976, no part of this publication may be reproduced, distributed or transmitted in any form or by any means or stored in a data base or retrieval system, without the prior written permission of the author.*

ISBN: 978-0-578-01449-4

## *Dedication*

*To my Dad who taught me (by example) how to have the drive and courage to succeed and to my Mother who taught me not to run over people in the process. Thank you!*

# TABLE OF CONTENTS

General Criminal Law Principles

**SPORTS VIOLENCE**

Illegitimate Sports Violence

Governmental Legislation

Internal League Controls:

Fans and Spectators

Sports Gambling

Sports Bribery and Game Fixing

Questions a Star College Player Might Ask about a Prospective Agent

Collective bargaining contracts

Family and Medical Leave Act

The Occupational Safety and Health Act of 1970

Workmen Compensation Statutes

Title VII of the Civil Rights Act of

Pregnancy Discrimination Act

Quid pro quo

Hostile working environment

Age Discrimination in Employment Act (ADEA

Americans with Disabilities Act

# I.   SPORTS CONTRACTS

Contracts in sports are no different than contracts in everyday life. Professional athletes are compensated for their services with a paycheck just as anyone else. This section examines the nature of personal services contracts of pro athletes. However, even the amateur athlete deals with important contract-related issues. Amateur athletes often have to make tough choices about changing their status from amateur to professional given the dramatic increase in money that may be available to be earned in their sports. Some professional athletes are paid a lot more money in one year than most people ever earns in their lifetimes.

**Sports Agents and Contracts**

Sports agents serve a valuable role in terms of securing and negotiating contracts for the professional athlete. Lawyers who represent athletes have generally been trained in the fundamentals of contracts and should be familiar with the current market value of their client relative to other athletes within the same sport. However, it should be noted that hiring a lawyer is not required (nor is an agent for that matter) to secure deals for the athlete. Some athletes do not wish to hire an agent for a variety of reasons, including having to pay commissions or other fees associated with the representation. Since the athlete has unique talents, abilities, and skills, their contracts are categorized as personal services contracts.

Technically, a personal service contract may not be assigned to someone else. An assignment is a transfer of rights that a party has under a contract to another person. Why can't a personal service contract be assigned? The talents of an athlete are unique. For example, Peyton Manning could not assign his contract to another player. His talents are so unique. The team owner would not honor such an assignment.

No one can be legally forced to work for someone for whom they do not want to work. The Thirteenth Amendment to the U. S. Constitution provides: *Neither slavery nor involuntary servitude, except as a punishment for crime whereof the party shall have been duly convicted, shall exist within the United States.* This provision of the Constitution has been interpreted as including a prohibition against requiring someone to work for an employer for whom they do not wish to work.

How then do team owners get away with trading players from one team to another, since this in effect is assigning a personal service contract? Any contract may be assigned *with permission* of the parties. The right to assign is part of a player's contract. However, some players have enough bargaining power to put in a *do not trade* clause. This keeps a team from assigning the player to a team for whom he does not want to play.

**Public Nature of Sports Contracts**

Though general contract principles apply in sports contracts, often such contracts are so important to the particular league or community, that each community has a vested financial and emotional interest in seeing their team perform well. Of course some sports do not receive the same sort of public exposure and generate the same widespread fan support.

## The Occupation of "Athlete"

The occupation of professional athlete has become recognized as one of the most financially rewarding professions. Sports sponsors often pay thousands of dollars to an athlete to promote its product. A sports contract can have an impact on the lives of thousands of people.

Today's amateurs must face crucial issues such as whether to continue to compete as an amateur or be lured away by money to professional teams during their sophomore or junior year of college. College sports such as football, basketball, baseball, and hockey are often regarded as proving grounds for the major professional leagues. Many athletes are urged to abandon amateur status to be compensated for their services as a professional.

Contracts for the employment of athletes should always be in writing and should contain covenants by the athlete like promising to refrain from certain acts, such as participating in dangerous activities.

## Matters to be considered in drafting contract for employment of athlete

The following is a checklist of matters to be considered in drafting a contract for the employment of an athlete:

- Names of parties.
- Addresses of parties.
- Statement of hiring.
- Term of contract.
- Duties and obligations of athlete.

- Attendance at training camp.

- Amount of compensation.

- Times at which compensation payable.

- Payment of bonus.

- Effect of taking bonus or bet on outcome of game.

- Board, lodging, and traveling expenses while traveling.

- Compliance with rules of the athletic association and/or club.

- Covenant not to play for others during term of contract.

- Covenant not to engage in related activities.

- Effect of not being in physical condition.

- Effect of injuries.

- Effect of temporary retirement from active sports.

- Payment of fines imposed by athletic association or club.

- Right of employer to assign the contract.

- Right of employer to seek injunction to prevent playing for others.

- Use of pictures for publicity purposes.

- Arbitration or other method of settling disputes between parties.

- Option to renew.

- Termination of contract.

- Grounds for termination.

- Procedure for termination.

- Incorporation of applicable rules and regulations of athletic association into

Contract.

- State's law to govern interpretation of contract.

- Effective date of contract.

- Date of execution of contract.

**General Contract Law Principles**

A contract is a legally binding agreement. A contract represents the meeting of the minds of the parties. Contracts in sports are subject to the same principles of contract formation as any other form of employment agreement.

There six elements that are necessary to a binding and enforceable contract:

- An agreement;

- Between competent parties;

- Based upon the genuine assent of the parties;

- Supported by consideration;

- Made for a lawful objective;

- In the form required by law.

Most sports contracts are *express contracts.* An express contract is a contract in which the agreement of the parties is evidenced by their words, whether spoken or written. There are virtually no more implied contracts in the sports industry. An implied contract is a contract in which the agreement is not evidenced by written or spoken words, but by the acts and conduct of the parties.[1]

## Agreement

It is essential to a contract that there be an offer and, while the offer is still in existence, it must be accepted without qualification. Once an offer is made, the person to whom it is made can respond in four ways:

- Accept;

- Reject (this automatically terminates the offer);

- Counteroffer (again, the offer is automatically terminated);

- Nothing (the offer then terminates after a *reasonable* time).

Offers may be terminated in any one of the following ways:

- Revocation of the offer by the person making it (the offeree);

- Counteroffer by offeree;

- Rejection of offer by offeree;

- Lapse of time;

- Death or disability of either party; or

- Performance of the contract becomes illegal after the offer is made. [2]

---

[1] For example, if you left your watch to be repaired and nothing was said with regard to how much you would be charged, you would be obligated to pay the reasonable value of the services, even though no specific agreement had ever been made. Of course, implied contracts are sometimes hard to prove.

[2] For example, if there is an offer made to sell alcoholic beverages to a store, but a city ordinance is passed prohibiting the sale of alcoholic beverages before the offer is accepted, the offer is terminated.

## Competent Parties

An issue can arise with regard to the legal "capacity" aspect of a minor signing a contract. Sports such as gymnastics, swimming, and tennis often involve contractual issues regarding minors. Satisfying this element may require the signature of a parent or guardian. Even though minors may enter into contractual arrangements, minors hold the ability to void such contracts at their option. However, if the contract is voided, the other party generally must be placed in the same position as prior to entering into the agreement, or at least at no worse position.

## Assent or Consent

The consent or assent of a party to an agreement must be genuine and voluntary. This assent will not be genuine or voluntary in certain cases of mistake, deception or undue pressure or duress. The agreement of parties may be affected by the fact that one or both of them made a mistake. A *unilateral* mistake is a mistake made by one party to the agreement. A mistake that is unknown to the other party usually does not affect the enforceability of the agreement.

A unilateral mistake of one party that the other party knows about may make the contract voidable by the party that is adversely affected by the mistake. A unilateral mistake regarding a *fact* does not affect the contract. For example, if a coach orders water-resistant parkas for his football team thinking that this means waterproof, he cannot get out of the contract unless the sale was made with some sort of misrepresentation as to the meaning of those words.

If both parties to an agreement make the same mistake

regarding a key factual matter, the agreement is *void.* For example, a contract is void if both parties mistakenly believe that the contract can be performed when, in fact, it is impossible to perform it.[3]

A person who has the ability and the opportunity to read a document before signing it is contractually bound by the terms of the document even if the person signed it without reading it. The signer cannot avoid liability based on the argument that no explanation was given to him of the terms of the contract. Even if a person is unable to read or understand the terms of the agreement, he is still bound by the terms of the agreement since he should have tried to obtain an explanation of the agreement. The exception to this rule is that if the other party knows, or has reason to know, that the signer cannot read nor has a limited education, some Courts would hold that the other contracting party should have read the document to the other party or explained the terms.

If a party relies on the explanation of another party as to the contents of the agreement, the contract may be voided under two circumstances: (i) the party was justified in relying on the explanation of the other party; and (ii) the explanation was fraudulent. The party making the explanatory statements does not have to be a lawyer, but can be any person who handles the agreement on a regular basis and therefore has a greater knowledge of the content than the other person.

---

[3] Suppose Smith promises over lunch to sell Jones an antique Mercedes in Smith's garage. Assume both parties believe the automobile is in Smith's garage. However, the car had been destroyed by fire an hour before the agreement and Smith had not learned of this. Since this fact was unknown to both parties, there is a mutual mistake as to the possibility of performing the contract. The agreement is therefore void.

## Supported by Consideration

Consideration is what the promisor (person making promise) demands and receives as the price for the promise. The *promisor* is the person making the promise, and the *promisee* is the person to whom the promise is made. Consideration consists of something to which the promisor is not otherwise entitled. It is not necessary to use the word *consideration* in a contract. Consideration is the price paid for the promise. When thinking of consideration, think in terms of legal value as opposed to economic value. While economic value (e.g., money) is the most common form of consideration, consideration does not have to involve money.

## Made for a Lawful Objective

The fourth element of a contract is that it must be made for a lawful objective. Courts will not enforce contracts that are illegal or violate public policy. Such contracts are considered void. For example, a gambling contract would be illegal in many states. If the illegal agreement has not been performed, neither party can recover damages from the other or require performance of the agreement. If the agreement has been performed, neither party can sue the other for damages or have the agreement set aside.

Assume Smith was not licensed to act as a sports agent. However, Jones asks Smith to help him procure a contract with a professional football team. Jones promises to pay Smith $10,000.00 if Smith can get him a NFL contract. Jones pays Smith $1,000.00 in advance. Smith successfully negotiates a contract for Jones with an NFL team. However, Jones refuses to pay the remaining $9,000.00. Smith sues Jones. A Court would most likely rule in favor of Jones as to the unpaid commission since the state's sports agent licensing statute was violated by Smith's acting as a sports agent without a license. The agreement to pay him a commission was therefore void and can not be enforced. Suppose Jones then claims that Smith should not be entitled to keep the $1,000.00 advance he had received. The Court would most likely hold that although Smith had no right to the commission, he had been paid and the Court would not aid either party to the illegal contract. Therefore, Jones could not recover from Smith the part of the commission that had already been paid.

## In the Form Required by Law

As a general rule, contracts may be either oral or written. However, the law requires a written agreement in specific situations. Most states have statutes that require the following types of contracts to be in writing or they will be unenforceable:

- An agreement that cannot be performed within one year after the agreement is made;

- Contracts involving the sale of land;

- The promise to answer for the debt of another person;[4]

- A promise by the executor or administrator of an estate of a deceased person to use personal funds to pay a debt of the estate;

- A promise made in consideration of marriage must be in writing (*e.g.*, a prenuptial agreement); and

---

[4] For example, an oral promise by the president of Acme Company to pay the debt owed by Acme to First National Bank would not be enforceable unless in writing.

- A contract provides for the sale of goods with a price of $500.00 or more.

## Interpretation of a Contract

If there is a dispute as to the interpretation of a contract, Courts seek to enforce the intent of the parties to the contract. The intent which will be enforced is what a *reasonable person* would believe that the parties intended. Sometimes the provisions of a contract are contradictory. In such a situation, a Court will try to reconcile the provisions and eliminate the conflict. However, if this cannot be done, the Court will declare that there is no contract. For example, John makes a contract to sell 100 acres of land to Joe. One paragraph of the contract states that the purchase price is $100,000.00. Another paragraph states that the purchase price is $1,100.00 per acre, which would produce a total price of $110,000.00. Which amount would be binding? Neither amount would be binding if the conflict in the terms could not be reconciled by *parol* evidence.[5]

In some cases, a conflict can be solved by considering the form of the conflicting terms. If a contract is partly printed or typewritten and partly handwritten, the handwritten part would prevail if it conflicted with the typewritten or printed part. If there is a conflict between the printed part and a typewritten part, the typewritten part would prevail. If there is a conflict between an amount or quantity expressed both in words and figures, as on a check, the amount or quantity expressed in words prevails. For example, if a check is written for $1,000.00, yet the check states it is for One Hundred and 00/100 Dollars, the words would prevail over the figures.

---

[5] Parol evidence is oral evidence, such as testimony in a court, as opposed to written evidence.

A contract is *ambiguous* when it is uncertain what the intent of the parties was and the contract is capable of more than one reasonable interpretation. Sometimes ambiguous terms can be explained by the admission of parol evidence. Also, Courts abide by the rule that an ambiguous contract is interpreted *against* the party who drafted it. In other words, the party who did not draft the contract will be given the benefit of the doubt so to speak.

## Categories of Contracts

Sports contracts can be divided into three general categories:

- professional services contracts (sometimes called standard player contracts)
- endorsement contracts, and
- Appearance contracts.

## Team Contracts versus Individual Contracts

If a professional athlete is part of a team, usually the athlete receives a standard Player's contract. The only difference between his contract and other members of the team are usually salary, bonuses, and the option to renegotiate.

## The Professional Services (Standard Player) Contract

The standard player contract (SPK) is usually in a "boilerplate" form. Boilerplate is standard wording that can be reused over and over without change. Whether the athlete is involved in a league with a players association or not, the contract usually offered to the athlete and other athletes are all the same other than the salary and bonus. There can be addendums to the SPK.

Newly formed leagues often model their own contracts after one of the Big Four

(NFL, MLB, NBA and NHL) in order to recognize issues relevant to team owners and athletes. Some start-up leagues, however, have taken a newer approach to professional services contracts by establishing minimal salaries for the athletes in that sport and rewarding the team and athlete on a per game basis with incentives. The now defunct Xtreme Football League (XFL), for example, offered modest salaries to its players. Such wages were comparable to wages of the average U.S. worker. This is primarily due to the fact that the league owned all of the teams rather than each team serving as a franchise for the league. None of the Big Four sports leagues are run by a single entity. Each team is a franchise and competes for players. That is a primary reason for the escalation of player salaries.

**Endorsement Contracts** Unlike the professional services contract, the endorsement contract does not involve an employer-employee relationship. Rather, it is one of contractor- independent contractor.[6]

An endorsement contract is one that grants the sponsor the right to use (i.e., license) the athlete's name, image, or likeness in connection with advertising the sponsor's products or services. In most professional sports, the

---

[6] An independent contractor is a person or business who performs services for another person pursuant to an agreement and is not subject to the other's control or the manner and means of performing the services. An independent contractor is distinguished from an employee, who works regularly for an employer. The exact nature of the independent contractor's relationship with the hiring party is important since an independent contractor pays their own Social Security, income taxes without payroll deduction, has no retirement or health plan rights, and often is not entitled to worker's compensation coverage.

leagues prohibit individual players from endorsing alcoholic beverages or tobacco products. Also, the NFL recently established a policy that players may not endorse certain nutritional supplements. There are no set rules for an endorsement agreement other than that they be legal. The more a sponsor feels that the athlete can assist in the sales of the particular product, the greater the likelihood of more money.

## Appearance Contracts

An appearance contract compensates the athlete for appearing at a public function, sports camp, golf tournament, etc.

## Drafting the Sports Contract

All professional services contracts have important common clauses. According to the standard player's contract of the NFLPA, MLBPA NBPA, and NHLPA,[7] all contract provisions have been established, except for salary and bonuses. Additionally, the players associations have group licensing arrangements in which players are compensated by licensing their names and likenesses in group package deals to trading card companies and video games.

It is important to remember that when drafting a contract, it is often a good policy to be a pessimist: Think of what can go wrong. Though most contracts begin as a beneficial relationship between the parties, it is well known that over time attitudes can change. Therefore, the contract drafter should use exceptional care to ensure that policies and procedures are provided to address situations and legal

---

[7] I.e., National Football League Players Association, Major League Baseball Players Association, National Basketball Players Association and National Hockey League Players Association.

issues that might arise when something goes wrong. Good contract drafters protect their client in the event such a situation might occur.

## Drafting Suggestions for a Sports Contract

The following clauses are pretty standard.

## Title

It is always important to name the agreement. Keep the description to a minimum, but the title identifies the type of contractual agreement. Phrases can be used such as Sponsorship Agreement, Sports Contract, Agreement for Athletic Services, or Representation Agreement.

## Describe the Parties

Establish the name and address of the parties to the contract. For example:

**Employment Agreement made *(date),* between *(Name of Employer)*, a corporation organized and existing under the laws of the state of *(Name of State),* with its principal office located at *(street address, city, county, state, zip code)*, the holder of a professional *(Name of Sport)* franchise of the *(Name of league) (Employer)*, and *(Name of Employee)*, of *(street address, city, county, state, zip code)*, *(Employee)*.**

## Term

It is always important to establish the duration of the agreement from the beginning date to the end date. For example:

**Subject to the provisions of the renewal options on the part of either party to this Agreement, as set forth below, the term of this Agreement shall begin on the effective date set forth above, and shall terminate on *(date)*.**

## Option of Club to Renew Contract

On or before *(date)* following the last playing season covered by this Agreement, Club may tender to Player an Agreement for the next succeeding season by mailing such Agreement to Player at his address as shown in this Agreement. If player does not sign and return such Agreement to Club so that Club receives it on or before *(date)* of that year, then this Agreement shall be deemed renewed and extended for a period of *(e.g., one year),* upon the same terms and conditions in all respects as are provided in this Agreement, except that the compensation payable to Player shall be the sum provided in the Agreement tendered to Player pursuant to the provisions of this section, which compensation shall in no event be less than _____% of the compensation payable to Player for the last playing season covered by this Agreement.

## Duties and Obligations

Once the parties, term of the agreement, and purpose have been established, it is important to outline the rights, duties, and responsibilities of each party. This can include compensation, but usually compensation has its own paragraph for clarification purposes.

Player's employment shall include attendance at training camp, playing the games scheduled for the team during the scheduled season, playing all exhibition games scheduled by the team during and prior to the scheduled season, and playing the play-off or championship series games for which Player is to receive such additional compensation as provided in this Agreement.

## Exhibition games

Exhibition games shall not be played on the *(number)* day prior to the opening of a team's regular season schedule or on a day prior to a regularly scheduled game. Exhibition games during the regular season shall not exceed *(number).* For the purpose of this section, invitational

**games shall not be considered as exhibition games.**

## Compensation

This is often referred to as *legal consideration.* An addendum attached to the contract is often helpful when using standard league contracts. The addendum could state increased salary, bonuses, and other incentives.

## Board, lodging, and travel expenses

**Club shall pay the reasonable board and lodging expenses of player incurred while playing in games for club in other than the home city of club. Club shall also pay all proper and necessary traveling expenses of player and his meals en-route to and from games.**

## Exclusivity

**Due to the personal and unique nature of the sports contract, most employers and sponsors require an exclusive arrangement . It is common for a sponsor in this paragraph to require the athlete to use the products or services exclusively at all times, especially in public, or the endorser may have the right to terminate the agreement as a breach of contract or failure to use "best efforts."**

## Participation in other sports

**Player and Club recognize that Player's participation in other sports may impair or destroy his ability and skill as a *(indicate sport)* player. Accordingly, player agrees, from and after the execution of this Agreement, and for the duration of this agreement, not to engage or participate in any other sport or activity involving a substantial risk of personal injury, including, but not limited to, automobile or motorcycle racing, fencing, parachuting or skydiving, boxing, wrestling, karate, judo, skiing, or ice hockey.**

## Confidentiality

A confidentiality clause is often considered valuable to both the team and the athlete. Players unions have somewhat undermined such a clause with respect to athletes under contract while represented by a players union by making salaries public. In nonunion contracts, confidentiality is an important consideration for the sponsor and the athlete to prevent similarly situated athletes from comparing their agreements. This will undoubtedly create concern for a party to the contract if the terms are revealed.

## Termination

If one party does not live up to its end of the bargain, he or she may be released from

the agreement. Topics covered in many termination clauses include:

- One party's refusal to keep the terms of the agreement confidential,

- The athlete's voluntary discontinuation of participation in the sport,

- Cases in which the athlete is found guilty of a crime or is found to have been a part of unethical or immoral conduct (sometimes called a *morals clause*).

- Participating in dangerous activities (e.g., skydiving, motocross racing).

## Grounds for Termination By Player

- If club defaults in the payments to player provided for in this agreement or fails to perform any other material obligation agreed to be performed by club under this agreement, player shall notify club in writing of the facts constituting such default or failure.

- If club shall not cause such default or failure to be remedied within (number) days after receipt of such written notice, player shall have the right, by a further written notice to club to terminate this agreement.

- On termination of this agreement by player, all obligations of both parties under this agreement shall cease on the date of termination, except the obligation of club to pay player's compensation to such date of termination.

## Non-assignment

It is important to establish that such an agreement is a personal services contract and therefore is non-assignable.

**The rights of each party under this Agreement are personal to that party and may not be assigned or transferred to any other person, firm, corporation, or other entity without the prior, express, and written consent of the other party.**

## Alternative Dispute Resolution (ADR)

The traditional method of resolving a breach of contract issue is through litigation. Alternative dispute resolution may be more effective in to resolving disputes by mediation or arbitration. Most collective bargaining agreements address issues related to arbitration and/or mediation. Arbitration is a process in which the disputing parties choose a neutral third person, or arbitrator, who hears both sides of the dispute and then renders a decision. Mediation is a process by which parties in a dispute negotiate a settlement of their claims against each other through the assistance of a trained, neutral mediator. It is a non-adversarial process. Mediation is entirely voluntary and non-binding. The mediator has no power to neither render a decision nor force the parties to accept a settlement. The mediator generally does not give an opinion or render an award, and typically does not even have any knowledge of the case prior to mediation.

The big difference between mediation and arbitration is that a mediator helps the parties to fashion their own settlement, while an arbitrator decides the issue. An arbitrator is more like a judge than a mediator. The parties go into arbitration knowing that they will be bound by the decision. The parties go into mediation knowing that nothing will be decided unless and until they agree to it. Arbitration, however, is unlike litigation in that the parties choose the arbitrator, the proceedings are conducted in a private manner, and the rules of evidence and procedure are informal. Also, in arbitration, the arbitrators tend to be experts in the issues they are called on to decide. Arbitration has been the widest used ADR process in the business world, and would be especially desirable where the parties do not want to litigate an issue, but do want a binding decision. They can go into arbitration knowing that they can get a quick, and relatively inexpensive decision, which they agree they will be bound by. Mediation offers no guarantee of a decision.

Most arbitration is binding. However, it can be non-binding if that is what the parties desire. That kind of defeats the purpose of arbitration though. In any event, in both binding and non-binding arbitration, the arbitrator renders a decision much like a judge.

It is not uncommon to find arbitration provisions in business contracts. An example of such a provision is as follows:

Any dispute under this Agreement shall be required to be resolved by binding arbitration of the parties hereto. If the parties cannot agree on an arbitrator, each party shall select one arbitrator and both arbitrators shall then select a third. The third arbitrator so selected shall arbitrate said dispute. The arbitration shall be governed by the rules of the American Arbitration Association then in force and effect

## Governing Law

Since many sports contracts affect parties from different states, agreeing upon the controlling law ahead of time can save jurisdictional issues from becoming problematic.

**This Agreement shall be governed by, construed, and enforced in accordance with the laws of the State of *(Name of State)*.**

## Merger

Merger is a legal term that essentially means that any other prior oral or written agreements or statements are null and void, and that this contract constitutes

the final and complete agreement between the parties.

**This Agreement shall constitute the entire agreement between the parties and any prior understanding or representation of any kind preceding the date of this Agreement shall not be binding upon either party except to the extent incorporated in this Agreement.**

**Signature Line**

Since many parties require possession of an original copy of the contract, signing in blue ink can avoid issues as to which contract is the original. Sometimes it is best to have the parties initial each page at the bottom to avoid later substitution of pages.

**Damages And Remedies For Breach Of Contract**

A contracting party may be entitled to damages if the other party breaches a contract. Generally, damages are the sum of money necessary to put a party in the same or equivalent financial position as the party would have been had the contract been performed.

A party may recover *compensatory* damages for any actual loss that the party can prove with reasonable certainty. An example would be in a situation where the plaintiff has paid $10,000.00 for a lawn tractor, but the defendant refuses to deliver the tractor. The *compensatory* damages would be $10,000.00.

*Punitive* damages are designed to punish. A Court uses punitive damages to make an example of a defendant in order to keep others from doing a similar wrong. Punitive damages are rare in a breach of contract case.

*Consequential* damages would arise in a situation where the failure to deliver the tractor caused the plaintiff to have to rent a tractor to cut the field. The amount of rent would be *consequential* damages.

A non-breaching party has a duty to *mitigate* damages. In other words, a non-breaching party has the duty to take reasonable steps to minimize damages. The failure to mitigate damages may cause the victim to only be allowed to recover damages that would have resulted if mitigated.

If Acme College refused to play a game it contracted to play with Southwestern State, and there was another school that could be substituted, like Northeastern State, the court would not award loss gate receipts to Southwestern State if they just sat on their hands and refused to try to get another team to fill that date. Damages would be the difference in probable gate receipts for an Acme College game and a game with Northeastern State.

An appropriate remedy for a breach may be *rescission* of the contract. This places the parties in the position they would have been had the contract never been entered into. For example, money is returned to the buyer and the buyer returns the merchandise to the seller.

*Specific performance* is an action to compel a party who breached a contract to perform the contract as promised. The subject matter of the contract must be unique, or an action for damages would be the proper remedy. Actions for specific performance are usually allowed with regard to:

- A contract involving the sale of particular real estate; and

- A contract for sale of a particular business.

Specific performance is not allowed regarding a contract for the sale of personal property unless the property is unique in some way like an antique, coin collection, or art objects. Generally, a party cannot obtain specific performance of personal service contracts or employment contracts. This is because of possibly violating the Thirteenth Amendment regarding involuntary servitude. However, breach of a service or employment contract can subject the breaching party to a suit for damages.

A contract may state the amount of *liquidated* damages to be paid if the contract is breached. Upon a party's breach, the other party will recover this amount of damages whether actual damages are more or less than the liquidated amount. Liquidated damages are damages specified in the contract itself and are often referred to as "agreed-upon" damages. For example, late delivery of jerseys to a school or team might have a clause that each day late constitutes damages of $100 per day. Courts will honor liquidated damage provisions if actual damages are hard to determine and the amount is not excessive when compared with probable damages. If the agreed-upon liquidated damage amount is unreasonable, the Court will hold the liquidated damage clause to be void as a penalty. In such situations, you have to prove the actual damages if the clause were declared to be void.

## NCAA Contracts and Amateurism

A sample policy on amateurism and the NCAA is as follows:

As a member of the NCAA, State University requires that all of its student-athletes be amateurs in their sport. You are a professional if you:

1.  Are paid (in any form) or accept the promise of pay for playing in an athletics contest;

2.  Sign a contract or verbally commit with an agent or a professional sports organization;

3.  Ask that your name be placed on a draft list (Note: in basketball, once you become a student-athlete at an NCAA school, you may enter a professional league's draft one time without jeopardizing your eligibility provided you are not drafted by any team

in that league and you declare your intention in writing to return to college within 30 days after the draft;

4.     Use your athletics skill for pay in any form (for example, TV commercials, demonstrations);

5.     Play on a professional athletics team; or

6.     Participate on an amateur sports team and receive any salary, incentive payment, award, gratuity, educational expenses or expense allowance (other than playing apparel, equipment and actual and necessary travel, and room and board expenses).

Though the National Collegiate Athletic Association (NCAA) is considered a nonprofit organization, its billion-dollar television contract and its rules and policies affect the sports industry in numerous ways and often present a conflict between the concepts of amateurism and professionalism.

The NCAA was originally established to address safety issues involved in the sport of football. The organization has grown to become the largest amateur organization in the United States related to the regulation of athletes. Membership in the NCAA is Divided into Division III, Division II and Division I, the largest division and the one that offers the most scholarships to athletes. Each sport has its own rules and limits the number of scholarships in a given sport. Sports such as football and basketball are characterized as "revenue" sports while soccer, gymnastics, track and field, and other sports are considered "non-revenue sports."

Membership in the NCAA is entirely voluntary, and some colleges or universities have chosen not to become a member of this organization. However, more than 1,200 schools are now members. Sharing in revenues generated by the NCAA is similar to a shareholder distribution plan. This "sharing of the wealth" is driven by television contracts with the organization for post-season football bowl championships and the contract with network television for the NCAA Division I Men's Basketball Tournament.

Recognizing that the professional sports industry and the minor leagues are now competitors in a sense for players, the NCAA has recently modified its rules regarding amateurism to allow a professional athlete to participate in a college or university sports program if the athlete has remaining eligibility, and the participation is in a different sport than the player's professional sport. Thus, a 27-year-old football quarterback who played professionally as a minor league baseball player may still be able to compete as an amateur in football for a college or university. It will be interesting to see if the NCAA changes its position further on "amateurism" in the near future.

## Evolution of Amateurism

An amateur athlete used to be defined as someone who participated purely for the love of the sport and did not expect compensation for athletic performance. For numerous years, the United States Olympic Committee (USOC) prevented professional athletes from participating in the Olympic Games just as the NCAA does not allow professional athletes to participate in college as amateurs within that particular sport. The USOC has modified its nonprofessional agenda, however, and actually endorses professionals to participate in its Olympic events. However, the NCAA continues to refuse to allow athletes to be paid for their services as athletes other than scholarships.

## Other NCAA Contract Issues

Numerous rules and regulations surround the athlete that signs and NCAA approved letter of intent. Athletes agree to rules that regulate transferring to another institution, being randomly tested for performance-enhancing drugs, and earning a minimum number of credit hours in their studies. These and other rules are important aspects of the contractual relationship between the NCAA and the athlete. The NCAA and USOC have agreed to examine ways to ensure that talented amateur athletes who have remaining collegiate eligibility may actually earn a stipend from an Olympic national governing body such as United States Swimming and still retain amateur status.

## Letter of Intent

Division I, Division II and NAIA[8] athletes are the beneficiaries of athletic scholarships (more specifically referred to as *grants-in-aid*). They sign an agreement with the college or university in the form of a letter of intent, which is a binding agreement between the athlete and an institution. This agreement provides that in exchange for the athlete's services in their sport, they will have tuition, room and board, and books paid for by the institution. However, no financial compensation may be awarded to athletes in exchange for their athletic talents in that particular sport.

There are questions, however, as to the validity of such agreements if a letter of intent were challenged in court. It appears that such an agreement need not be signed as a

---

[8] National Association of Intercollegiate Athletics

prerequisite to participation in NCAA-governed sports, though the NCAA manual does refer to the letter of intent program. The National Letter of Intent Program is actually not administered by the NCAA but rather through the College Commissioners Association (CCA). The CCA has administered this program for 30 years and has no reported lawsuits against it. However, hundreds of appeals are filed each year with respect to letters of intent, particularly when prospective athletes sign to play with a college or university and the coach who recruited them is no longer employed at the college when the athlete later enrolls in school. He or she may desires to transfer to another school.

Many letters of intent are signed by high school seniors who may not have reached the age of 18. Therefore, the legal capacity of the minor might be taken into consideration if he or she desires to void this agreement

## Health Club Contracts

Most states now regulate the terms of a health club contract in some form or another. Many states have limits on the length of health club contracts. Many states cap the length of a health club contract to no more than three years. Many states also allow the member to void a health club contract within three business days of signing the contract. Due to the extremely competitive nature of health club contracts and the temptation for fraud, health club regulations often are found within a particular state's consumer protection laws and may include a mandatory warning on the contract in bold lettering such as:

**YOU, THE BUYER, MAY CANCEL THIS TRANSACTION AT ANY TIME PRIOR TO MIDNIGHT OF THE THIRD BUSINESS DAY AFTER THE DATE OF THIS TRANSACTION. SEE THE**

ATTACHED NOTICE OF CANCELLATION FORM FOR AN EXPLANATION OF THIS RIGHT.

**Links to Sports Contracts on the Website of U.S. Legal Forms, Inc.**

**Representation Agreement Between Sports Agent and Athlete**

http://www.uslegalforms.com/us/US-01702BG.htm

**Employment Contract Between College and Coach of College Sports Team**

http://www.uslegalforms.com/us/US-01710BG.htm

**License Agreement For Use of Land for Sports Playing Field**

http://www.uslegalforms.com/us/US-01723BG.htm

**License Granting Use of Land for Playing Baseball, Softball or Soccer**

http://www.uslegalforms.com/us/US-01244BG.htm

## II.  TORT LAW AND WAIVERS

Conduct that harms other people or their property is generally called a *tort*. It is a private wrong against a person for which the person may recover damages. The injured party may sue the wrongdoer to recover damages to compensate him for the harm or loss caused. The conduct that is a tort may also be a crime. A *crime* is a wrong arising from a violation of a *public duty*. A tort is a wrong arising from the violation of a *private duty*. Again, however, a crime can also constitute a tort. For example, assault is a tort, but it is also a crime. A person who is assaulted may bring charges against the assailant and have him prosecuted criminally and may also sue the assailant for damages under tort law. An employee's theft of his employer's property that was entrusted to the employee constitutes the crime of embezzlement as well as the tort of conversion.

There are three types of torts: intentional torts; negligence; and strict liability. An *intentional tort* is a civil wrong that occurs when the wrongdoer engages in intentional conduct that results in damages to another. Striking another person in a fight is an intentional act that would be the tort of battery. Striking a person accidentally would not be an intentional tort since there was not intent to strike the person. This may, however, be a negligent act. Careless conduct that results in damage to another is *negligence.*

Generally, liability because of a tort only arises where the defendant either intended to cause harm to the plaintiff or in situations where the defendant is negligent. However, in some areas, liability can arise even when there is no intention to cause harm or negligence. For example, in most states, when a contractor uses dynamite which causes debris to be thrown onto the land of another, causing damages such as broken windows, the landowner may recover damages from the contractor even though the contractor may not have been negligent and did not intend to cause any harm. This is called *strict liability* or *absolute liability.* Basically, society is saying that the activity is so dangerous to the public that there must be liability. However, society is not going so far as to outlaw the activity.

*Products liability* is major area of sports tort law. Participants use all different types of sports-related equipment. Products liability refers to the liability of any or all parties along the chain of manufacture of any product for damage caused by that product. This includes the manufacturer of component parts, an assembling manufacturer, the wholesaler, and the retail store owner. Product liability suits may be brought by the purchaser of the product or by someone to whom the product was loaned. Products liability claims can be based on negligence, strict liability, or breach of warranty of fitness.[9] In a strict liability theory of liability, the degree of care exercised by the manufacturer is irrelevant. If the product is proven to be defective, the manufacturer may be held liable for the harm resulting from the defect.

---

[9] Under the Uniform Commercial Code (UCC), which has been adopted in some form by almost all states, there are implied warranties in every sales transaction that the goods sold are fit for the ordinary purposes for which such goods are to be used.

**Negligence**

Negligence is the failure to follow the degree of care that would be followed by a reasonably prudent person in order to avoid foreseeable harm. A person can be negligent if he or she acts with less care than a reasonable person would use under similar circumstances.

Ben drove a car on a country road at 35 miles an hour. The maximum speed limit was 45 miles an hour. He struck and killed a cow that was crossing the road. The owner of the cow sued Ben for the value of the cow. Ben raised the defense that since he was not driving above the speed limit, there could be no liability for negligence. Was this defense valid? No. A person must at all times act in the manner in which a *reasonable person* would act under the circumstances. The fact that Ben was driving within the speed limit was only one of the circumstances to consider. The weather or the condition of the road may have made it unreasonable to drive at 35 miles an hour. Driving slower than the speed limit does not in and of itself prove that the driver was acting reasonably. The reasonable person standard varies in accordance with the situation. Generally, when a jury is involved, what is reasonable are what members of the jury believed is reasonable.

The degree of care required of a person is that which an ordinarily prudent person would exercise under similar circumstances. This does not necessarily mean a degree of care that would have prevented the harm from occurring. This degree of care varies. For example, if one is engaged in a service involving skill (such as a medical doctor) the care must be measured in light of what an ordinarily prudent skilled person (e.g., doctor) would be. The question the jury seeks to determine is what care and skill would reasonably be expected under the circumstances involved in the case. Plaintiff must prove that:

- The defendant owed a duty of care to the plaintiff;

- The defendant breached that duty to the plaintiff;

- The conduct of defendant was unreasonable;

- The defendant was the proximate cause of the breach of duty; and

- There is evidence of damages.

If the plaintiff fails in proving any of these points, the plaintiff's claim should not succeed.

In order for someone to be legally responsible for damages, it is necessary to show that the wrongful act was the cause of the harm. The legal term is that the act must be the *proximate cause* of the harm.

The final element of negligence is damages. A plaintiff may recover monetary damages to compensate the plaintiff for economic losses such as lost wages and medical expenses. A plaintiff may also recover non-economic losses such as for pain and suffering. Punitive damages may also be appropriate. Punitive damages are designed to punish the defendant for his wrongdoing and are generally only appropriate if the plaintiff can prove gross negligence or willful misconduct.

## Contributory Negligence versus Comparative Negligence

If the negligence of the plaintiff is partially responsible for his harm, his recovery from the defendant may be reduced or barred. This is called *contributory* or *comparative* negligence. In a small minority of states, the contributory negligence rule states that if the plaintiff contributes to his harm, he cannot recover from the defendant. In most states, this rule has been rejected because it has been regarded as unjust in situations where the plaintiff's negligence was slight in comparison to the defendant's negligence.

Comparative negligence provides that there should be a comparing of the negligence of the plaintiff and the defendant. This is the rule followed in most states. The negligence of the plaintiff would not bar recovery in these states, but would only reduce the plaintiff's recovery to the extent that the harm was caused by plaintiff. For example, if the jury decides that the plaintiff has sustained damages of $100,000.00, but that his own negligence was one-fourth the cause of the damage, the plaintiff would only be allowed to recover $75,000.00.[10]

*Assumption of risk* is a defense which a defendant can raise which basically states that the plaintiff has knowingly assumed the risk of the harm that was caused. A fan hit by a basketball at a basketball game has assumed the risk of getting hit because it is a known danger that basketballs sometimes go into the stands because of a bad pass or if a player misses a pass.

**Gross Negligence**

What happens when sports participants break the rules so badly that it appears the sole purpose of a player was to injure another player intentionally during a game?. This level of recklessness is difficult to prove. However, if the

---

[10] Some states combine the contributory and comparative negligence rules and refuse to allow the plaintiff to recover anything if his negligence is more than 50% of the cause of the harm.

plaintiff is successful, the plaintiff may recover punitive damages for the outrageous conduct of the defendant in addition to the general damages (e.g., medical bills and loss of wages).

## Spectator Injuries

While most sports torts involve personal injuries caused by participants against each other, a spectator to a sporting event might be injured. Some examples are foul balls, deflected hockey pucks, and flying debris (at a Nascar event). In such an event, who is responsible for the spectator's injuries? Does the owner of a stadium have a duty to warn or protect spectators from foul balls or other foreseeable injuries? American courts have refused to allow recovery for injuries to spectators caused by the open and obvious rules of the game, particularly when it comes to foul balls. On the other hand, what about other sports, such as golf, hockey, and football when an activity on the field might impact the fans in the stands (e.g. fights between spectators)? Does an owner of a stadium owe a duty to spectators to prevent all foreseeable injuries, or does common sense impose some duties on the spectators themselves? Do cities and counties have to warn recreational swimmers that diving into shallow water could expose them to a risk of danger? It is wise to post signs that warn of potential dangers but to warn of all possible dangers are clearly not possible in the sports context. If a sign is at issue, the adequacy of the posting of the sign is usually the focus of the analysis.

In 2002, a 13-year-old girl died after she was hit in the head by a hockey puck that shot over the glass during the Columbus Blue Jackets NHL hockey game in March 2002. She died two days after she was hit. The ticket stubs had warnings about the dangers due to flying pucks. It is unlikely that such warnings provide an absolute defense to death from flying pucks.

When large crowds gather for sporting events, there is a greater likelihood of injuries to spectators. Balancing fun, safety, and security have been an issue for organizers of events for many years.

A person who operates a place of public amusement or entertainment must exercise reasonable care with regard to the construction, maintenance, and management of his buildings or structures and his premises, having regard to the character of entertainment given and the customary conduct of persons attending such entertainment. The operator must employ sufficient personnel to maintain the premises in a reasonably safe condition. He or she must use ordinary care to maintain the floors and aisles along which patrons are expected to pass in a reasonably safe condition for their use; and this principle has been applied in cases where personal injury resulted from a slippery floor, aisle, ramp or walkway, defective carpet, or the presence of an object the floor or in the aisle.

*Res ipsa loquitur* is a Latin term meaning *the thing speaks for itself*. It is a doctrine of law that one is presumed to be negligent if he/she had exclusive control of whatever caused the injury even though there is no specific evidence of an act of negligence, and the accident would not have happened without negligence. The traditional elements needed to prove negligence through the doctrine of res ipsa loquitur include:

- The harm would not ordinarily have occurred without someone's negligence;

- The instrumentality of the harm was under the exclusive control of the defendant at the time of the likely negligent act; and

- The plaintiff did not contribute to the harm by his own negligence.

The *res ipsa loquitur* doctrine has been applied in actions for injuries caused by the falling of various objects in theaters or other public places of amusement or exhibition, including:

- The fall of an object or substance from the ceiling;

- The striking of a traveler on the public streets by a baseball which came over a fence surrounding a baseball park.

- The striking of a fisherman in the eye by his or her fishing companion while the latter was casting.

In some cases involving defective seats or the collapse of a seat, bleachers, grandstands, a balcony, or the like, it has been held that the doctrine of *res ipsa loquitur* was applicable, or at least that such a happening warranted the inference that the plaintiff's injury was caused by the negligence of the defendant.

Since the doctrine of *res ipsa loquitur* generally is limited to those cases where it appears that the instrumentality which caused the injury was under the sole and exclusive control and management of the defendant, the courts have, as a general rule, refused to apply the doctrine where injury resulted from the pushing, crowding, or jostling of other patrons.

**Wrongful Death**

When somebody dies in consequences of a wrongful act a

person, either by negligence or by a deliberate act, such a death is called *wrongful death.* This is the civil equivalent of the criminal charge of one of the forms of homicide, including murder. Should a sports participant be held liable for the death of another athlete or a spectator? Virtually all sports involve an activity and an aspect of risk that could lead to the death of a participant. It is important for architects and administrators to provide protective screening and appropriate warnings for participants and spectators related to such concerns. What about fights? What about slugging someone in the face with a hockey stick?[11]

## Malpractice in Sports

Malpractice is a failure by an physician or other professional to use the care and skill that other members of their profession would use under similar circumstances. When an accountant, doctor, attorney, or some other professional contracts to perform services, there is a duty to exercise skill and care as is common within the community for persons performing similar services. Failure to fulfill that duty is malpractice. What about team physicians and trainers. What if a trainer or doctor employed by a team rather than the player recommends that the injured player participate? To whom does the medical practitioner owe a duty of care, the player or the team? Sometimes this decision is not clear cut. Malpractice is a broad category and could involve anything from an improper diagnosis to the prescription of an inappropriate medication.[12]

---

[11] *Sports Law* at p. 69 by Adam Epstein, Delmar Leaning (2003)
[12] *Id.* at p. 76

## Sports Officials

Another area of sports torts involves the officials of games or other sports contests. Officials in sports can greatly affect the outcome of the sports contest. Professional sports such as football, basketball, and hockey have incorporated the use of the television replay to ensure that the often subjective regulation of the sports contest remains as objective as possible. Sports officials, however, are often subject to harassment, intimidation, and sometimes violent, physical or verbal abuse from fans, players, and coaches. Whether at the professional or amateur level, sports officials are often the targets of hostile emotions due to the extreme competitiveness in the sports arena. Due to numerous lawsuits against sports officials for alleged intentional misconduct, states have been forced to enact laws that protect officials and provide immunity from such lawsuits. Immunity from civil suits only applies to unintentional, negligent acts by the officials. This affords the sports official some protection against litigation.[13]

## Workers Compensation

For most kinds of employment, state **workers' compensation statutes** govern compensation for injuries. The statutes provide that the injured employee is entitled to compensation for accidents occurring in the course of employment. Every State has some form of workers' compensation legislation. The statutes vary widely from State to State. When an employee is covered by a workers' compensation statute, and when the injury is job connected, the employee's remedy is limited to what is provided in the worker's compensation statute.

---

[13] *Sports Law* at p. 77 by Adam Epstein, Delmar Leaning (2003)

Compensation for injuries to an athlete is a prime subject for any collective bargaining agreement in professional sports that involve a players association or union When players are injured from an activity arising out of and in the course of their employment, the private agreement between the players, team, and league often avoid any necessity of filing a claim under the state's workers compensation statute.

Since being an employee is a prerequisite to filing a claim under workers compensation, usually only professional athletes may consider filing a claim. Should student-athletes who receive athletic scholarships be entitled to compensation if they suffer a temporary or permanent injury while participating in their sport for their school, college, or university? It seems clear that the student-athlete has not yet been given the right to claim workers compensation since they are not yet recognized as employees. However, the NCAA has a Catastrophic Insurance Plan covering every student who participates in college sports, including managers, trainers, and cheerleaders. One can learn more about this plan by visiting the NCAA website (www.ncaa.org). [14]

**Insurance**

Since any sports activity involves a degree of risk or injury, it is generally recognized that events and participants should purchase insurance to protect against a claim of negligence arising from that activity. Sports insurance policies do not relieve an individual or event from liability from negligent behavior. However, having insurance does ensure that if a judge or jury believes that damages should be awarded for an injury arising from the activity, the

[14] Id.

insurance company stands in the shoes of the defendant and must therefore pay in accordance with terms of the insurance policy. Exceptional student-athletes and professional athletes are wise to purchase a policy that covers their own participation in the activity. Such insurance for the professional athlete may be referred to as a career-ending injury insurance and usually requires large premiums to maintain because of the potential for great financial loss, especially at the professional level.

## Waivers and Releases

A *waiver* or *release* is the intentional and voluntary act of relinquishing something, such as a known right to sue a person, educational institution, or organization for an injury. Waivers and releases are commonly used by the sponsor of an event (*e.g.,* a marathon) and schools when competitors, students, faculty, or visitors participate in a private or institution-sponsored activity. The term *waiver* is sometimes used to refer a document that is signed before any damages actually occur. A release is sometimes used to refer to a document that is executed after an injury has occurred. A waiver can be an effective way for a person, educational institution, or organization to inform students, parents, event participants, and family members of the risks involved in various activities and to shield the person, educational institution, or organization from liability. The best releases explain the risks of a particular activity or program in detail. So, even if all aspects of a release are not upheld in court, you can show that the releasing party was informed about the specific risks and should be responsible for his or her own conduct. Waivers, as described above, often contain express assumption-of-risk language. This type of language:

- Describes the activity;

- States that the signer has full understanding of the nature of the document;

- Knows of the specified risks;

- Voluntarily chooses to assume the risk; and

- Agrees not to hold the institution liable for the consequences of his or her participation in the described activity.

If the participant later is injured and brings a lawsuit, this language permits an organization, school, college, or university to maintain that the participant's signature shows he or she voluntarily took part in an activity with known risks and, therefore, should not receive damages. When outside entities or organizations use an institution's facilities (such as a school's track or cross country course), the institution may try to limit its liability exposure by having participants sign a hold-harmless agreement. This document is a promise by one party not to hold the other responsible for any costs or claims that may result from a loss that results from the subject matter of the agreement.

**CAVEAT:** Courts go not always uphold waivers and releases. In *Quinn v. Mississippi State University*, 720 So. 2d 843 (Miss. 1998), the Mississippi Supreme Court rejected a release signed by a 12-year-old attendee at a Mississippi State University baseball camp and the child's father. The child and his parents sued the institution for injuries the child sustained when he was hit in the mouth with a baseball bat by a coach who was demonstrating how to hit baseballs off a tee. Because the release did not mention an instructor's acts, the court ruled that it was not clear that the parties contemplated such acts of negligence when they signed it. In *Whittington v. Sowela Technical Institute,* 438 So. 2d 236 (La. 1983), the Louisiana Court of Appeals upheld a jury verdict against the institute on the grounds that the release was not freely and voluntarily given. A senior nursing student was required to sign the document before participating in a field trip to a hospital. On the way to the hospital, the driver of the 15-passenger van in which she was a passenger lost control and the van turned over, killing her. Among the factors the court considered were that the institute did not offer alternative classes for students who chose not to participate in the field trip, that it required students to travel in a group and did not permit them to use their own vehicles, and that it dictated the terms of the document. Students were required to sign to release it from liability for a reasonably foreseeable danger.

Some courts have upheld releases and waivers. In *Sharon v. City of Newton,* 769 N.E.2d 738 (Mass. 2002), the Massachusetts Supreme Judicial Court upheld a school district's release signed by a student and her father to permit her participation in cheerleading activities. The student was injured while participating in cheerleading practice, and the court rejected the lawsuit alleging negligence and the negligent hiring and retention of the cheerleading coach. In reaching its decision, the court noted that the student and her father had ample time to read and understand the release before signing it, that cheerleading activities were not deemed to be compelled nor were essential, and that releases favored as a matter of law in Massachusetts. It stated that to hold releases unenforceable in such circumstances would expose public schools, which offer many extracurricular sports opportunities, to financial costs and risks that would inevitably lead to reductions in those programs. As these examples show, courts vary in their approach to releases depending on the particular facts of each case, the releases effect on other statutes and laws, and the courts' views of the benefits of releases as a matter of public policy.

**Essential to the Public**

Courts have often ruled that waivers and similar documents that affect the public interest are invalid. In *Kyriazis v. University of West Virginia*, 450 S.E.2d 649 (W. Va. 1994), a student at the University of West Virginia who signed a release as a condition for playing in a rugby club sued the institution after being injured during a match. The university argued that the rugby club was an extracurricular activity and not a public or essential service, but the court said that providing recreational activities were part of the university's educational mission and of its performance of a public service. However, state courts differ in what they deem to be essential.

**Voluntary Agreement**

Courts have rejected agreements when they find that the participants do not enter into the activity, freely, and voluntarily, as was the case in *Whittington v. Sowela Technical Institute*.

**Parties to an Agreement**

Many courts will invalidate documents signed on behalf of minors. For example, in *Scott v. Pacific West Mountain Resort*, 834 P.2d 6 (Wash. 1992), the Washington Supreme Court rejected a release that the mother of a 12-year-old boy had signed, saying it violated public policy and was unenforceable because it barred the child's own cause of action. The child had been seriously injured at a ski school when he crashed while trying to ski on a slalom race course.

## Unambiguous Language

Releases and similar documents are most likely to hold up in court if they use specific, clear, and unambiguous language. Releases for a specific event are more likely to survive legal scrutiny than releases for a more long-term activity. Some courts have rejected documents that don't explain the nature of the activity, including its difficulty, dangers, location, and other details. Some jurisdictions require use of the word *negligence,* or similar such words. Courts may also require that the language which describes what is being waived be conspicuous, such as in bold or capital letters.

## Relative Bargaining Power

Courts usually examine whether the two parties to an agreement have equal bargaining power. The courts may take into account a number of factors, including the opportunity for the two parties to negotiate. For example, in *Kyriazis v. University of West Virginia, supra,* the court took into consideration that the university's counsel prepared the form, but the student did not have the benefit of counsel.

## Gross Negligence and Intentional Acts

Courts do not permit institutions to waive their responsibility when they have exercised gross negligence or misconduct that is intentional or criminal in nature. Such an agreement would be deemed to be against public policy because it would encourage dangerous and illegal behavior.

## Ticket Stubs and Waivers

Waivers are often found on the backside of ticket stubs for sporting and entertainment events. Most fans do not read these waivers (many are not even aware of the existence of the waiver on the back). Defendants will often raise as a defense to a negligence claim that such language should relieve them from liability. Generally, these waivers are virtually unenforceable since there was no intent on the part of the fan to agree to such terms. Also at issue is the lack of informed consent, and the courts have traditionally refused to impose such waivers on fans as a matter of public policy.[15]

## Minors and Waivers

In areas such as Little League sports or even amusement park rides, waivers are often signed by parents of a minor to avoid liability or give up the right to sue in the event of an accident that causes injuries. The law is unclear as to whether parents who sign waivers on behalf of their children will release a potential defendant from liability to the minor. The trend is to enforce such waiver arrangements signed by parents on behalf of a child. However, it is quite possible that a court could refuse to enforce such a waiver, especially for gross negligence or recklessness. A court does have the option of not enforcing a waiver signed by the minor or parent. Such cases should be analyzed on a case-by-case basis, paying close attention to the particular state's common law interpretations of waivers.[16]

---

[15] *Id* at p. 79
[16] *Id* at p. 79

## Commercial Misappropriation

Though athletes may find that a successful suit under defamation standards is extremely difficult, an area that proves worthy of a lawsuit involves the use of the athlete's name, image, or likeness without the athlete's consent in order to make a profit or sale. Such non-approved use of an athlete's persona is referred to as commercial misappropriation.

Since manufacturers and other sellers of products and services commonly use an athlete in marketing in the form of an endorsement contract, athletes must be cognizant to protect from the unauthorized misuse of their image. Establishing a trademark (including an Internet domain name) for one's name or image may be necessary for professional athletes (and certainly professional and amateur leagues and organizations) to prevent improper use of a name for profit.

## Products Liability

Products liability in sports represents an area of negligence involving a sporting goods. When plaintiffs sue a manufacturer of sporting goods, the claimants allege that they suffered an injury due to the use of a product that was defective. Bats, gloves, shoes, helmets, pads and other goods used in a sport are subject to a lawsuit if there is a defect in the design or manufacturing process. This may be referred to as a manufacturing defect or design defect.

Manufacturers of goods may also be sued for failing to warn the user of potential dangers involving use of the product. Since goods are involved, the Uniform Commercial Code (UCC) is often called into play, and the user of the product alleges that there was a breach of the warranty of merchantability or a breach of the implied warranty of fitness for a particular purpose. UCC Article 2 governs the sales of goods and has been adopted in whole or in part by every state.

**Links to Sports Contracts on the Website of U.S. Legal Forms, Inc.**

**Waiver and Release from Liability for Soccer Training**

http://www.uslegalforms.com/us/US-00628BG.htm

**Waiver and Release by Parent of Minor Child from Liability for Soccer Training in favor of Soccer Organization and Instructors**

http://www.uslegalforms.com/us/US-00680BG.htm

**Waiver and Release by Parent of Minor from Liability for Wrestling Training**

http://www.uslegalforms.com/us/US-00752BG.htm

## III.  SPORTS CRIMES

Rules of law set the standard of conduct for people to follow. When a person disobeys a law, he is susceptible to two possible consequences. One consequence is punishment by the government for his crime, and the other is the possibility of a civil lawsuit for damages sustained by the victim of the crime. Damages sustained by a victim are governed by principles of tort law. A crime is an offense against the government. It is a breach of a duty to the public. It is conduct that is prohibited and punished by a government. Each state has its own set of statutory criminal laws. However, these statutes are very similar. Crimes may be classified in terms of their seriousness as felonies and misdemeanors. An act may be a felony in one state and a misdemeanor in another. Felonies include serious crimes such as arson, murder and robbery, for example. Crimes not classified as treason or felonies are misdemeanors and include such things as reckless driving and disturbing the peace. Felonies are generally regarded as more serious in nature. Felonies require a penalty of more than one year in state or federal prison.

Misdemeanors, though still serious, do not allow for incarceration for more than one year in county jail. State and federal laws both fall into misdemeanor and felony categories. Crimes against the person including assault, battery, robbery, hazing, murder, rape, and kidnapping. Crimes against property rights include arson, trespass, vandalism, and theft. Crimes affecting the public health and welfare including blackmail, illegal gambling, and prostitution. Crimes against the government including tax evasion, treason, RICO violations, and terrorism. There has been debate as to whether or not a sports participant may or should be charged with a crime for activity that occurs during a sports contest. Should athletes be subject to such criminal charges during a sports contest for their misconduct or is this better left up to the sports leagues and organizations themselves? Very few cases involving these types of sports crimes have ever gone to court.

High-profile athletes lead a life in the public spotlight and may often be held to higher scrutiny for their behaviors both on and off the field than the general public. However, should such financial and social status affect whether a prosecutor brings a charge against sports participants for intentionally injurious conduct during a sports event?

Violent and aggressive contact among sports participants provides a vicarious thrill for the crowd, and such behavior is generally perceived to be a legitimate part of the game, not a matter for criminal courts. Still, violence in the sport of hockey has been prosecuted in Canadian courts.

**Types of Crimes**

Criminal law is certainly a factor to be considered in sports. For example, numerous federal and state laws outlaw the use of certain performance-enhancing drugs, sports gambling, ticket scalping, sports bribery, and the influence of organized crime in sports. Additionally, sports agents who fail to register with the appropriate state agency or those who offer financial inducements to a student-athlete may be subject to criminal and civil penalties for such actions. Much of the violence found in sports would constitute crimes against the person if it occurred outside the sports contest. Players hit, punch, check, trip, and commit other aggressive and violent acts during the course of a sporting event. Such conduct is usually considered part of the game, but occasionally the conduct is so outrageous that a criminal charge might be warranted. Some states are adopting legislation to address intentional injuries to sports participants, particularly sports officials.

## Contact Sports

Athletes in contact sports are trained to be aggressive and are often encouraged to make violent plays even as children. In the sports of football, hockey, and boxing, for example, participants are encouraged from a young age to hurt the opponent. Clearly, this is the ultimate goal of boxing.

Are hockey players encouraged to use their sticks as potentially deadly weapons? Are football players taught to hit each other by leading with their head and hitting a vulnerable opponent? Should the aggressive and sometimes out-of-control behaviors by athletes during a sports contest be subject to criminal law?

## General Criminal Law Principles

*Burden of Proof:* Prosecutors who believe that illegal behavior has occurred during a sports contest must prove their criminal case beyond a reasonable doubt. This is more difficult than the preponderance of evidence test in tort law. It is more difficult to prove that a defendant is guilty of a crime than liable in tort. If the defendant is found guilty of a crime, the judge must then render a sentence. Most criminal laws dictate a minimum and maximum sentence, and the judge must consider mitigating factors that might reduce a sentence.

## Defenses to Criminal Charges

The defenses to crimes of consent to contact, self-defense, and a general reluctance by the federal and state government to prosecute alleged crimes have limited the exposure of criminal law in the sports context. Additionally, if a player reasonably fears imminent harm by an opposing player, the defense of self-defense can often overcome the prosecution's attempt to show intent to injure.

## Criminal Intent

The essence of criminal law is that the perpetrator has formed an intent to commit a crime and then carried out that intent. Such intent is referred to as the *mens rea,* and the act itself is called the *actus reus.* Both elements are necessary for most criminal convictions. A person cannot be punished for having criminal thoughts alone. However, the crime of conspiracy does punish wrongdoers for agreeing to commit a future crime. Additionally, if an individual attempts to commit a crime and fails, he or she may be punished; attempted murder is one example. In other words, the attempt was a crime even though it failed. To get a criminal conviction, the prosecutor generally has to prove that the defendant had the intent to commit an unlawful act.

## Assault and Battery

The crimes of assault and battery would likely be the most prevalent crimes in sports. An assault is a willful attempt or willful threat to inflict injury upon another person. It is also defined as intentionally placing someone in fear of imminent bodily harm. A battery is the actual intentional physical contact. It is sometimes referred to as a successful assault. When an assault and/or battery involves a weapon, serious bodily injury, deadly force, or when the assault or battery is committed in conjunction with another crime, the term aggravated is often used.

## SPORTS VIOLENCE

It was in American football that athletic violence was first questioned on a governmental level. In 1901, six American university football players died while playing in games. The press of the day condemned the deadly violence that had occurred and demanded changes in the sport. University presidents threatened to end all collegiate contests. In 1905 The President of the United States, Theodore Roosevelt, a former collegiate boxer at Harvard University, stepped in and forced collegiate officials to change the rules of football to protect the players. He threatened to stop all football playing if the rules were not changed and implemented by the next season. Roosevelt prevailed, and American football survived its first threat.

### Illegitimate Sports Violence

In contact sports players often suffer injuries. However, at what point (if any) does an injury as the result of honest play turn into an injury due to intentional and excessive use of force by a player that might subject him to criminal liability? Much of the analysis of the criminal law application in sports context comes from hockey and the Canadian courts. Currently only a few major cases appear to set a standard for prosecuting athletes for violence sorts. Where the line is drawn between acceptable (within the rules) and unacceptable (outside the rules) violence remains unclear. In 1969, Wayne Maki of the St. Louis Blues hockey team swung his stick at Boston Bruins player

Ted Green and fractured his skull in a preseason exhibition game in Canada's capital of Ottawa. Both players were involved in two fights in the same game, and both were thereafter charged with different forms of assault. Maki's case was dismissed under the theory of self-defense, but the court refused to differentiate between sports contests and real-world violence. In the Green case, Green was found not guilty because it was held that his actions were an involuntary reflex to be part of the roughness of the game. No conviction resulted in either case, but the court noted that sports were not immune from criminal prosecution. One famous case in the United States involving the NHL followed a 1975 incident involving Dave Forbes, a player for the Boston Bruins. Forbes knocked down an opposing player and proceeded to punch him in the back of the head, and pummel his head into the ice. This was the first U.S. case where a player was criminally prosecuted for on-ice violence. Although the evidence was overwhelmingly against Forbes, he was nonetheless acquitted by a split jury decision. Alarmingly, from the time of this incident until today, the criminal court system within the U.S. has deferred to league self regulation within hockey.

## Hackbart v. Cincinnati Bengals, Inc.

Though this was not a criminal case, the court discussed the involuntary reflex defense regarding aggressive contact during a sports contest. Cincinnati Bengals football player Charles Clark hit Denver Broncos player Dale Hackbart on the back of the head out of frustration after an interception. The play was over, and Hackbart was not looking when he was hit from behind. He broke three vertebrae in his neck and suffered several muscular injuries as a result. The district court stated, "The violence of professional football is carefully orchestrated. Both offensive and defensive players must be extremely aggressive in their actions, and they must play with reckless abandonment of self-protective instincts."[17] The 10th Circuit Court of Appeals reversed the trial court by holding that even a football player may be held responsible for injuring an opponent if he acts with the reckless disregard for the opponent's safety.[18]

## The Case of Dino Ciccarelli

In another hockey case, Dino Ciccareffi, the captain and all-time leading scorer for the Minnesota North Stars, pounded Luke Richardson in the mouth repeatedly. In 1988, a Canadian court held that Ciccarelli was guilty of criminal assault and had to serve one day in jail and pay a $1,000 fine as an example to others that such violence in hockey is not acceptable. This was the first ever jail sentence for a professional athlete for violence that occurred during a sports event. Other cases have been prosecuted, but they have been limited to hockey and have been tried mostly in Canadian courts. Ciccarelli is believed to be the first National Hockey League player to receive a jail term for an on-ice attack on another player.[19]

## February 21, 2000 – Marty McSorley Incident

One of the most publicized incident of excessive violence in the modern era of hockey is that involving Marty McSorley of the Boston Bruins, and Donald Brashear of the Vancouver Canucks on February 21, 2000. After fighting and losing to Brashear early in the contest,

---

[17] *Hackbart v. Cincinnati Bengals, Inc.,* 435 F. Supp. 352, 355 (D. Co. 1977), rev'd 601 F.2d 516 (10th Cir. 1979), cert. denied 444 U.S. 931 (1979).
[18] *Id* at p. 92
[19] *Id* at p. 93

McSorley sought revenge later in the game by trying to goad Brashear into another fight, which Brashear would have no part of. With time winding down, and his team significantly behind, McSorley skated towards Brashear from behind and slashed at his head with his stick. Brashear's head smacked the ice, sending him into convulsions. The NHL immediately suspended McSorley for the remainder of the season. Later, he was convicted of assault and given an 18-month conditional discharge by the court.

Criminal assault occurs when one unjustifiably and intentionally uses force upon another with intent to cause injury. The crime usually involves a threat of harm, coupled with improper contact with the other person. As every fan knows, ice hockey involves considerable body contact and occasional fighting. Many consider the hits, blows and fights as a part of the game. The NHL has rules regarding penalties for such infractions. Over the years, many have been hurt in hockey altercations, but few cases have gone to criminal court. The *McSorley* case did.

### March 8, 2004 – Todd Bertuzzi Incident

Late in the third period, while losing 8-2, Vancouver's Todd Bertuzzi stalked Colorado's Steve Moore down the ice holding onto the back of his jersey. Bertuzzi could be seen whispering into Moore's ear, while he leisurely strolled behind him. When the play began to move in the other direction and Steve Moore began to skate away, Bertuzzi dropped his stick and delivered a blindsided, right handed, punch to the side of Moore's face. Moore fell forward with Bertuzzi still on his back driving his head into the ice. Several other players quickly joined the melee by piling on top of Moore's motionless body. Steve Moore suffered facial lacerations, a concussion, and two damaged vertebrae, which have subsequently put his professional hockey career on hold, indefinitely. Bertuzzi was immediately suspended by the NHL for this transgression, while the Vancouver police immediately opened a criminal investigation.

The legal response to this incident was so immediate that police officers began interviewing fans, players, trainers, coaches, and administrative personnel who were in attendance. On June 24, 2004, Todd Bertuzzi was formally charged by the Vancouver attorney general for assault causing bodily harm. Due to the publicity and severity of the act, along with the overwhelmingly public outcry that followed, it is speculated that all athletes in the NHL were quickly informed of the incident and the severity of the punishment that Todd Bertuzzi was facing.

Another incident involved Jesse Boulerice, who while playing in a minor league hockey game "grabbed his hockey stick at the end of the handle with both hands, and swung his hockey stick, in a baseball type swing, at Andrew Long." Similar in substance to the McSorley incident, the victim here hit the ice and went into convulsions. However, the injuries suffered in this case were more severe than those reported in McSorley. Following the path of the NHL, the Ontario Hockey League (OHL) suspended Boulerice for a year. In addition, Boulerice was suspended from the Philadelphia Flyers minor league team (to which he was assigned) for six months. Also, formal assault charges were filed against Boulerice by Long in Wayne County, Michigan. Originally charged with assault with intent to commit great bodily harm, Boulerice was able to plea to a reduced charge of aggravated assault, no trial was held, and he was sentenced to 3 months probation. Although deterrence for players as a result of the court's action in this case is not likely, the league suspension of one year and six months will certainly have a greater impact in that regard. Despite the noted increased prosecution indicated above, to this day, no player in the NHL or its minor league affiliates has been sent to jail for conduct in an athletic event that occurred on U.S. soil.

Over the past decade or so, the courts have begun to convict players more frequently for on-ice assault. And, where the courts initially differentiated between conduct that was incidental to the game and in the heat of the moment (Maki), with conduct occurring after the play was over (Gray), recent court decisions are now simply finding incidents that occur during the course of play to be excessively violent. Since the most common defense to excessive violence is consent, the court in *Regina v. Cey*,[20] developed a five part test to determine if valid consent exists in the context of an athletic event. They are: "(1) Nature of the game; (2) nature of the act; (3) the degree of force employed; (4) the degree of risk of injury; and (5) the state of mind of the accused."

## Governmental Legislation

Certain individual or collective conduct during a sports contest would likely be prime targets for criminal charges if they occurred outside the sports arena. However, prosecutors rarely charge athletes for acts committed during a game. Many people believe that leagues themselves should regulate violence in sports. There have been several attempts at the federal level to regulate

---

[20] *Regina v Cey* (1989), 48 C.C.C. (3d) 480 (Sask. CA.) 32.

sports violence, such as proposal of The Sports Violence Act of 1980. This act would have imposed up to one year in prison for professional athletes who knowingly used excessive force during a game. However, it failed to gain enough votes. Another proposed act, the Sports Violence Arbitration Act of 1983, failed to create a sports court for excessive violence.[21]

## Internal League Controls

Violence in sports has become so prevalent that professional sports leagues and other governing bodies have had to police such activity themselves and provide punishment (i.e., penalties). In some sports, a stick or ball could conceivably be used as a deadly weapon to seriously hurt an opponent. Most spectators and prosecutors believe that such activity is just part of the game. Some scuffles and plays are so violent, however, that professional and amateur sports leagues have had to form rules that penalize players with fines and suspensions.

Hockey, for example, recognizes a variety of penalties and even a penalty box for transgressors. A player may be penalized for numerous violations, including boarding, butt-ending, charging, clipping, cross-checking, elbowing, fighting, high-sticking, holding, hooking, kneeing, roughing, slashing, spearing, and tripping.

Baseball winks at bench-clearing brawls. Pitches intended to bean the batter, will result in the pitchers ejection. Managers may be thrown out of a game for confrontations with the umpire. Football imposes penalties for roughing the passer and kicker, unnecessary roughness, holding,

---

[21] *Id* at p. 91

spearing, and tripping. These acts would constitute criminal and civil assaults and batteries but for their occurrence during a sports contest. One of the major objections to leagues controlling violent behavior is that their actions have not gone far enough. When fines or suspensions are handed down, they often have little impact to athletes who make millions for their sports prowess.

## Fans and Spectators

Sometimes sports fans may have to be controlled when watching a sports contest. It is quite common for fans during the heat of a contest to become violent in the stands among each other and against sports officials and even athletes. This phenomenon is not unique to the United States. In fact, it is generally accepted that the most violent fans in the world are at soccer matches. A large number of fans have died during pre- and post-game soccer celebrations.[22]

In the city of Philadelphia, fans became so disruptive that when the Philadelphia Eagles football team plays home games at Veterans Stadium, a roving municipal court is located literally underneath the playing field. A local municipal judge hears cases involving disorderly conduct, public intoxication, and other offenses.[23]

## Sports Officials and Crimes

Numerous examples of players, parents, and other spectators attacking referees and umpires have forced states to enact legislation to protect sports officials from violence. Many states have tort laws related to the protection of sports officials.

---

[22] *Id* at p. 93
[23] *Id*

## Ticket Scalping

Ticket scalping is the process of legitimately purchasing a ticket (or large numbers of tickets) from a legitimate source and then reselling the tickets on the street for more money than the legitimate price. Some States have adopted laws regulating ticket scalpers and provide for civil and criminal penalties. Scalping can be a highly profitable business, particularly when the event is in high demand.

## Sports Gambling

*Sample College Policy*

A student-athlete is not eligible to compete if he/she knowingly:

- Provides information to individuals involved in organized gambling activities concerning intercollegiate athletics competition,

- Solicits a bet on any intercollegiate team,

- Accepts a bet on any team representing the institution,

- Solicits or accepts a bet on any intercollegiate competition for any item (e.g., cash, shirt, dinner) that has tangible value, or

- Participates in any gambling activity that involves intercollegiate or professional athletics, through a bookmaker, parlay card, or any other method employed by organized gambling

In 1992 Congress enacted the Professional and Amateur Sports Protection Act that prevents states from sponsoring sports-based betting other than in Nevada, Oregon, Delaware, and Montana. Since gambling often involves interstate commerce, Article I of the U.S. Constitution allows the federal government to regulate this activity. Sports gambling involves professional and amateur contests. Gambling can be addictive, a danger to the emotional and financial well-being of the gambler. Sports gambling is a major concern on college campuses. The NCAA has amended its own rules to address the problems and issues related to sports betting.

## Sports Bribery and Game Fixing

The basis for the concern about sports gambling is that games fixed by players, coaches, trainers, or others defeat the ideal that the outcome of a sporting event is left to chance and skill. An important issue in professional and amateur sports is the role that the athletes, coaches, and even sports officials themselves might play in altering the outcome of a game in order to profit from betting on a loss, victory, or point spread. Federal legislation and numerous state laws have addressed the issues of fixing games and point-shaving, especially after the gambling scandals involving athletes in the 1990s. Federal and state legislation guards against bribery in sports contests by providing for fines and/or imprisonment. [24]

## Professional Sports Gambling Incidents

In 1919, eight Chicago White Sox baseball players were allegedly involved in a conspiracy that fixed the World Series, and all the players were banned for life. The White Sox players, including Shoeless Joe Jackson, became known as the Black Sox. In 1982, the Baltimore Colts football team selected Art Schlichter as the fourth overall pick in the NFL draft. The Colts did not know that

---

[24] *Id* at p. 96

Schleicher had a compulsive gambling addiction, and he was ultimately suspended by the NFL for betting on sports. He has been in jail frequently for his misconduct. Another notable victim of gambling impropriety is baseball player Pete Rose. Rose's alleged gambling problem led Major League Baseball to ban him from eligibility to baseball's Hall of Fame. [25]

## Amateur Sports

College athletes have become targets for illegal gambling activities, particularly since student-athletes are not paid for their services. Additionally, there have been recent attempts to outlaw all betting on any Olympic, college, or other amateur sports nationwide. More than $500 million is wagered on intercollegiate sports each year in Nevada.[26]

## College Incidents

In October 1951, three University of Kentucky players were arrested for taking bribes to shave points in a game in New York's Madison Square Garden two years earlier. In November 1981, Rick Kuhn and four others were found guilty and sentenced to jail for game fixing. Kuhn was a member of the Boston College basketball team. In 1995, Kevin Pendergast, a placekicker from Notre Dame placed a bet of $20,185 in Las Vegas that Northwestern University's basketball team would lose to the University of Michigan by 25.5 points. Pendergast, along with Dewey Williams and Dion Lee (both Northwestern players), agreed to shave points in exchange for money. All three were found guilty and sentenced to prison.[27]

---

[25] *Id* at p. 97
[26] *Id*
[27] *Id*

# IV. SPORTS AGENTS

Historically speaking, most sports agents recognize the inception of the profession stemming from the work of several individuals during the 1960's. However, sports agency can actually be traced back to 1925 when Red Grange hired an agent to negotiate his professional football contract. Red Grange was the first football player to have a personal representative, an agent as they are called now, to work out a performance contract. Grange was the first professional athlete in team sports whose pay was linked with the number of fans his fame and performance attracted to the games. These have become commonplace for professional athletes. Grange did not go out for football when he went to the University of Illinois. He was a star in four sports in high school (track, football, basketball and baseball). He thought baseball and basketball were his best sports bets to earn a varsity letter. When his fraternity brothers directed him to go out for football and got out the big paddle, Grange decided to report. He was issued jersey No. 77. In the first scrimmage against the Illinois Varsity, Grange returned a punt 65 yards for a touchdown. Before Grange's meteoric career on the gridiron, college football was largely a campus game of interest to students and alumni; but by the time Grange's All-American career was finished at the University of Illinois, millions who had no particular interest in a college were aware of the Galloping Ghost and college football. Professional football, before Grange, was largely played by teams from neighboring towns in sand lot circumstances before hundreds, rather than thousands of fans.

Grange's 1923 team turned in an unbeaten season, were co-champions of the Big Ten and Red Grange, in his first varsity year, was named an All American. Something very special was arranged for the 1924 season. The new University of Illinois Memorial Stadium, largest campus arena in the nation for football, was to be dedicated on October 18. The University of Michigan, who was also undefeated in 1923 and co-champions with Illinois, would be the opponent. Michigan came to the big game a favorite. Illinois was missing some of its players from the 1923 team through graduation. Illinois had also lost its first game of the season, 9 to 6, to the University of Nebraska.

Grange ran ninety-five yards for a touchdown on the opening kickoff and then rushed from scrimmage for three more touchdown runs of sixty-seven, fifty-six and forty-four yards before leaving the field with three minutes remaining in the first quarter. In the second half, he scored a fifth TD on a twelve-yard run just for good measure.

On Nov. 22, 1925, the day following his last game for the University of Illinois, Red Grange signed the first big time professional contract, casting his lot with the Chicago Bears, It called for one hundred thousand dollars and a share of the gate in a period when most professional football players were getting twenty-five to a hundred dollars a game, if they were paid at all.

In the 1960s, attorney Mark McCormack's work with young golfer Arnold Palmer probably changed the manner in which sponsors dealt with professional athletes. Since the 1960's, many other remarkable sports agents have made an impression on the profession that is now dominated by high-profile individuals working for large sport management agencies. In a famous scene in the 1996 film *Jerry Maguire,* the sports agent played by Tom Cruise is goaded by his client, played by Cuba Gooding Jr., to repeatedly scream into the phone "Show me the money." By the time that film came out, however, the role of the sports agent had long since been transformed into one far more sophisticated than simply negotiating contracts. And while screenwriter Cameron Crowe based the Jerry Maguire character on agent Leigh Steinberg, it was Mark McCormack who ushered in the modern era of sports management and marketing. McCormack, founder of International Management Group (IMG), believed the popularity and marketability of athletes could transcend borders, cultures, language, even sports itself. McCormack-managed athletes were the first to endorse clothing, watches, and motor oil. They played exhibition matches around the world. They gave inspirational talks to business at a hefty price tag.

Whether it was setting up golf matches between a young Arnold Palmer and company executives at $500 a game, arranging tennis exhibitions throughout China featuring Bjorn Borg and Jimmy Connors, or promoting a soccer match between Pele's New York Cosmos and the soccer star's former Brazilian teammates, McCormack had a gift for keeping his clients well-known and well-paid.

McCormack was born in Chicago in 1930 When he was just 6 years old he was hit by a car and suffered a fractured skull. The doctors said contact sports like football and basketball were out, so golf became McCormack's passion. He starred in the sport at the College of William & Mary, and one day came up against a pretty good Wake

Forest golfer -- Palmer. The two hit it off, and it was not long before McCormack, after obtaining a law degree from Yale, was busy helping Palmer and other pro golfers look over their contracts. In 1960, after a hand-shake management deal with Palmer, McCormack was on his way. After Palmer came deals with South Africa's Gary Player and Jack Nicklaus, giving McCormack a lock on golf's "Big Three." He then branched into tennis and other sports with a global footprint. By 1985, IMG's roster included golfer Palmer, soccer's Pele, tennis players Martina Navratilova and Chris Evert Lloyd, skier Jean-Claude Killy (who became a very close friend of McCormack's), runners Sebastian Coe, Bill Rodgers, and Mary Decker Slaney, baseball star Jim Rice, and football player Herschel Walker. Athletes knew that at IMG, they stood a good chance of earning just as much off the playing field as on and that IMG would manage everything, from negotiating with team owners to investing their money to making sure they got to appointments on time.

McCormack himself took an intensely personal interest in many of the athletes. Besides lasting friendships with Palmer, Killy, and hundreds of others, McCormack later in his career became a father figure for other athletes, including tennis star Monica Seles. In 2003 McCormick died at age 72.

One need not be a lawyer to be a sports agent, but many agents are lawyers. As a general rule, student-athletes with remaining eligibility may not have an agent to represent their interests in that particular sport. Agents are notorious for becoming occasionally overzealous in furthering the athlete's interests to secure a contract with a team or league. There is no typical, formal education program for sports agents. Many sports agents have law degrees. Others have no formal college education. Those who attend college earn degrees in a variety of fields, including legal studies, political science, sociology, and sports management.

Practically speaking, however, obtaining a law degree has become an unwritten prerequisite to break into the profession in terms of maintaining a competitive advantage. One can become an agent without a law degree, but being a lawyer allows you to earn money practicing law while building up your sports agency practice. It takes some start up money to be a sports agent to compete with big firms that often give potential clients all sorts of cash and gifts. Agents without formal legal training will likely continue to recruit clients as long as those agents find athletes that will let them represent them. Ultimately, the most important issue for sports agents is to keep their clients happy.

Though there are no current federal laws that directly governs sports agency, this may change in the near future. Uniform Athlete Agents Act (UAAA) is a model act governing sports agents. It was written by the National Conference of Commissioners on Uniform State Laws. It is available for adoption by states. A sports agent advocates and represents the legal and business affairs of a professional athlete, usually for a fee. This fee is usually a percentage of the athlete's income that came from negotiations by the Agent. The NFL regulates this percentage. Generally speaking, the term sports agent refers to someone who tries to get an athlete to let him represent him when in negotiations with professional teams.

Agents have a *fiduciary* relationship with their clients. A fiduciary is someone who owes a duty of loyalty to safeguard the interests of another person or entity. Fiduciary duty is a legal requirement of loyalty and care that applies to any person or organization that has a fiduciary relationship with another person or organization. A fiduciary duty is one of complete trust and utmost good faith.

As stated earlier, there are no specific qualifications to become a sports agent. In recent years, however, numerous states have attempted to define and ultimately regulate sports agents and their activities. The National Football League Players Association (NFLPA) now requires a four-year college degree from an accredited institution in order to represent professional football players in the National Football League (NFL). In the major professional sports leagues of the NFL, Major League Baseball (MLB), National Basketball Association NBA) and National Hockey League (NHL), players associations serve as unions and actually regulate fees that the agent may charge the player. These players association are powerful and are capable of barring the agent from being able to represent players within that sport for a violation of its policies and procedures. Agents are now required to pay expensive fees to the players associations. These costs can discourage a new agent from entering the profession.

Agency law has existed for hundreds of years. The basis of this law is for one person to allow another person to act on his behalf. An agency relationship is one in which one party (an agent) agrees to act on behalf of another (the principal). Examples could be a sales clerk, a sports agent, or the president of a corporation. Employees are oftentimes agents of their employers, but this is not always true. A sports agent, for example, is not an employee of his client, but is an agent of his client. The sports agent would be an independent contractor. An employee who acts within the scope of his/her employment furthers the business interest of the employer by creating a relationship that would hold the employer responsible for the actions of the employee. The phrase scope of employment is often referred to as respondeat superior, a Latin phrase meaning let the master answer. An agent expressly enters into an agency agreement with a principal to further the interests of that principal. Sports agents serve in this capacity.

Until the enactment of the Uniform Athlete Agent Act (UAAA) there were too many different state laws governing or regulating sports agents. Such laws theoretically required that agents register and pay fees in each and every state in which they recruited student-athletes. Additionally, differing definitions of sports agent and student-athlete caused great debate on the need for a uniform federal law. Adoption of the UAAA may end this debate.

The National Collegiate Athletic Association has made it clear that having an agent is akin to relinquishing one's amateur status. In recent years, the NCAA has allowed a student-athlete to participate as an amateur in one sport while remaining a professional (with an agent) in another sport.[28] It does not appear that the NCAA at this time is

---

[28] Chris Weinke, one of the finest quarterbacks in Florida State history, signed with Florida State out of high school and spent four days in August of 1990 on the FSU campus before signing a professional baseball contract with the Toronto Blue Jays. He spent six years in the Toronto Blue Jays organization before returning to Florida State in the spring of 1997. In 1999, he led Florida State to its second National Championship and first undefeated season.

willing to allow a student-athlete to have an agent and still participate in intercollegiate athletics in that particular sport. With the advent of television, professional sports became more visible. Television meant the influx of more money into sports. More money meant players forming unions and wanting more of the pie. Cable and satellite television continues this trend, and sports agents followed the money and have served as advocates for professional athletes rights.

Requiring a sports agent to be a lawyer would allow for more regulation over agents with the ability to take a law license away. However, the advent of the UAAA may be a better way to regulate sports agents.

Some states have enacted laws governing contracts made between athletes and athlete agents, which vary by state. Such laws may govern issues such as state registration and recordkeeping of athlete agents and disclosure requirements in their agency contracts. The majority of states have enacted the Uniform Athlete Agent Act (UAAA). The UAAA requires an agent to provide important information to enable student-athletes and other interested parties to better evaluate the prospective agent. The UAAA also requires that written notice be provided to institutions when a student-athlete signs an agency contract before his or her eligibility expires. In addition, the UAAA gives authority to the Secretary of State to issue subpoenas that would enable the state to obtain relevant material that ensures compliance with the act.

Alabama is serious about its amateur sports and in order to maintain the legitimacy of its amateur sports it is has adopted the Alabama Uniform Athlete Agents Act (the "Act"). Essentially, the Act requires any agent doing business in Alabama to register with the state. It also contains certain restrictions upon the activities that an agent can and can't engage in. Alabama adopted its Act in the current form in 2001, and is one of approximately 30 states that have adopted similar acts. For example, in addition to requiring the agent to register with the State, the Act states that an agent may not *(1) Give any materially false or misleading information or make a materially false promise or representation. (2) Furnish, directly or indirectly, any thing of value to a student-athlete before the student-athlete enters into the agency contract. (3) Furnish, directly or indirectly, any thing of value to any individual other than the student-athlete or another registered athlete agent.* [Alabama Code § 8-26A-14(a)]. It also goes on to state that a student-athlete may not, *(2) Accept anything from an athlete agent without first entering into a contract in conformity with this chapter.* (Alabama Code § 8-26A-14(d)).

In addition to regulating the conduct of agents, the Alabama statute prescribes significant criminal penalties for both student-athletes and agents that do not follow the terms of the Act. Section 8-26a-15 of the Alabama code makes a violation of the Act by an agent a class B or C Felony, depending on the type of violation. Class B Felonies can carry a sentence of up to 20 years, while Class C convictions can be up to 10 years. Violations by student-athletes are Class C misdemeanors and carry a mandatory minimum sentence of 70 hours community service. While it is highly unlikely that a single incident would result in a 20 year prison sentence for an agent, the point is that Alabama clearly wasn't messing around when it created the Act - and it didn't stop there. Alabama also provides civil remedies to universities who are harmed by the actions of the agent and student-athlete. Alabama Code § 8-26A-16(B) allows the university to recover "losses and expenses incurred because . . the educational institution was injured by a violation of this chapter or was penalized, disqualified, or suspended from participation in athletics by a national association for the promotion and regulation of athletics, by an athletic conference, or by reasonable self-imposed disciplinary action taken to mitigate sanctions likely to be imposed by such an organization."

## Questions a Star College Player Might Ask about a Prospective Agent

First make sure that the agent is registered with the state .

- Did you graduate from Law School? If so, where and when did you graduate?

- Why does it matter whether my future agent went to Law School?

- What is your educational background?

- What is your professional background?

- Have you ever been disbarred, suspended, reprimanded, censured, or otherwise disciplined or disqualified as an attorney, or as a member of any other profession?

- Are there currently any complaints or charges pending against you regarding your conduct as an attorney or as a member of any profession?

- Have you ever been investigated or found guilty of any violations of NCAA rules or those of a professional organization? If so, when and what were the charges?

- Do not hesitate to ask around about a prospective agent's reputation. Ask the player association of your sport, ask other athletes, even ask other agents.

- Do you have ownership interests in your company? Are you a partner or strictly an employee?

- What services do you offer to your clients other than contract negotiations? (financial planning, tax advice, etc.)

- Make sure your needs are met and that the agent is not overextended in the process.

- Who will be negotiating my contract?

- Can you provide me with a list of current clients?

- How many clients have you lost and what were the reasons for their leaving?

- Can you provide me with their phone numbers? (for privacy reason they may not be permitted to provide past clients contact information but it doesn't hurt to ask and it would benefit you to know the reason the client left from the client's prospective).

- Consider what it means to you to work with an agent whose clients have stayed with them for the player's entire career.

- Have you ever had a dispute with a client and if so, how was it resolved?

- Who do you consider to be your top clients?

- What have you done to advance the careers of your clients off the field?

- What will you do for me once I decide I no longer want to play professionally?

- Do you provide an annual statement to your clients? Can you provide me with an example?

- How do you keep your clients informed of charges?

- What is your fee structure?

- Are fees negotiable?

- How and when are you to be paid?

- Are you bonded? (if your agent will be handling your money this is important)

- What is the duration of the agreement?

- What are the procedures for terminating the agreement?

- What happens to the agreement if I do not make the team; if I am waived; or if I get injured?

- What kind of insurance is provided to players?

- Can you provide me with a projection of my draft status?

- If I am a free agent, how can you help maximize my chances of making a team?

Be careful when dealing with a prospective agent who is willing to offer you money, gifts or other inducements to encourage you to sign with him or her; this will impact your eligibility, not theirs. Always interview more than one agent to ensure that you understand the process and are comfortable with your future decision.

## Oklahoma Application for Registration of Athlete Agent

http://www.uslegalforms.com/ok/OK-SOS-FM-92.htm

## Representation Agreement Between Sports Agent and Athlete

http://www.uslegalforms.com/us/US-01702BG.htm

# V. EMPLOYMENT LAW

The relationship of an employer and an employee exists when, pursuant to an agreement of the parties, one person, the employee, agrees to work under the direction and control of another, the employer, for compensation. The agreement of the parties is a contract, and it is therefore subject to all the principles applicable to contracts. The contract may be an express contract. In other words, the duties of the employee will be specifically set forth in the contract. The contract may also be implied. Most employment contracts are implied oral agreements. In this type of arrangement, the employer is accepting the services of the employee that a reasonable person would recognize as being such that compensation would be given to the employee.

Collective bargaining contracts govern the rights and obligations of employers and employees in many employment relationships. These occur when a union negotiates on behalf of employees. Collective bargaining involves representatives of the employees bargaining with a single employer or a group of employers for an agreement. This agreement will cover such things as wages, hours, and working conditions for the employees. The employees, of course, make up a union and elect members to represent, and negotiate for, them with the employer.

The National Labor Relations Act (NLRA) guarantees

employees the right to form a labor union and requires employers to deal with a duly-elected union as the bargaining agent for the employees. The NLRA prohibits employers from interfering with employees and from discriminating against an employee as a result of the employee's union activity. In most instances, an employment contract will not state its expiration date. In such a case, the contract may be terminated at any time by either party. However, the contract may expressly state that it will last for a specified period of time such as a contract to work as a general manager for five years.

Ordinarily a contract of employment may be terminated in the same manner as any other contract. If it is to run for a definite period of time, the employer cannot terminate the contract at an earlier date without justification. If the employment contract does not have a definite duration, it is *terminable at will.* This is called employment at will. Under the employment at will doctrine, the employer has historically been allowed to terminate the contract at any time for any reason or for no reason. Some State Courts and some State Legislatures have changed this rule by limiting the power of the employer to discharge the employee without cause. For example, Court decisions have carved out exceptions to this doctrine when the discharge violates an established public policy, such as discharging an employee in retaliation for insisting that the employer comply with a federal or state law. Courts may sometimes construe an employer's statements concerning continued employment as a part of the employment contract, and therefore require good cause for the discharge of an at-will employee. Also, written personnel policies used as guidelines for the employer's supervisors have been interpreted as restricting the employer's right to discharge at-will employees without just cause. Employee handbooks or personnel manuals have been construed as part of the employee's contract. This is why all personnel manuals and employee handbooks should contain a disclaimer. A sample disclaimer would be: "This employee handbook is not intended to create any contractual rights in favor of you or the company. The company reserves the right to change the terms of this employee handbook at any time."

The Fair Labor Standards Act (FLSA), also known as the Wage and Hour Act, requires payment of a minimum wage as well as the payment of overtime after 40 hours of work per week. Payment of overtime is to be 1-1/2 times the regular hourly rate. This Act also deals with child labor laws. Generally, children under the age of 14 are not supposed to work. Children between the ages of 14 and 16 can work in all industries with the exception of certain hazardous work.

Certain exemptions are available under the FLSA to executives, administrative and professional employees, and for outside salesmen. Generally, employees without work through no fault of their own, are eligible for unemployment compensation benefits. Unemployment compensation is provided primarily through a federal and State system under the unemployment insurance provisions of the Social Security Act. State agencies are loosely coordinated under this Act. Basically, States are generally free to prescribe the amount and the length of benefits and the conditions required for eligibility. In most States, the unemployed person must be available for placement in a similar job and be willing to take such employment at a comparable rate of pay. If an employee quits a job without cause, or is fired for misconduct, he ordinarily is disqualified for unemployment benefits.

The Family and Medical Leave Act (FMLA) is a federal act that entitles employees of an employer with 50 or more employees to up to 12 weeks of unpaid leave during any 12 month period for the following reasons:

- birth or adoption of a child;

- to care for a spouse, child or parent with a serious health problem; or

- a serious health problem of the employee that makes the employee unable to do his or her job.

To be eligible for this leave, an employee must be employed by an employer for 12 months or more and have worked at least 1250 hours during the 12 months prior to the leave.

The Occupational Safety and Health Act of 1970 (OSHA) was passed in order to insure, as much as possible, safe and healthy working conditions for employees. OSHA provides for establishing safety and health standards and for enforcement of these standards. The Secretary of Labor has been granted broad authority under OSHA to write occupational safety and health standards. Any person adversely affected by these regulations of the Secretary of Labor can challenge their validity in a U.S. Court of Appeals. The Secretary's standards will be upheld if they are reasonable and supported by substantial evidence. The Secretary must show a need for a new standard by showing that it is reasonably necessary to protect employees against a significant risk of material health impairment. The Secretary also must show that the standard is economically feasible.

## Workmen Compensation Statutes

For most kinds of employment, state workers' compensation statutes govern compensation for injuries. The statutes provide that the injured employee is entitled to compensation for accidents occurring in the course of employment. Every State has some form of workers' compensation legislation. The statutes vary widely from State to State. When an employee is covered by a workers' compensation statute, and when the injury is job connected, the employee's remedy is limited to what is provided in the worker's compensation statute. In other words, the employee cannot sue his employer for negligence. Generally, no compensation is allowed for a willful, self-inflicted, injury, or one sustained while the employee is intoxicated.

**Title VII of the Civil Rights Act of 1964** (which was substantially amended in 1972 and 1991) prohibits terminating an employee or refusing to hire an applicant for a reason which amounts to discrimination because of race, color, sex, religion or national origin. The Act prohibits disparate treatment which is treating one employee less favorably than another because of race, sex, etc. The Act also prohibits disparate impact situations. This would be an employment practice which was neutral on its face (e.g., height requirement), but had a disparate impact on a protected class (e.g., women). Such policies must be justified by a bona fide job necessity. Certain tests which an employer might give to a job applicant might be found to be culturally biased and therefore have a disparate impact against a minority. This is not to say that all tests will be declared illegal by a Court. However, a test must have a reasonable relation to the job for which it is to be used. *Word of Mouth* hiring can also cause disparate impact.

**The Pregnancy Discrimination Act** requires that an employer treat pregnancy in the same manner that other disabilities are treated. Women that are temporarily disabled by pregnancy or childbirth must be provided with the same benefits as other disabled workers. This includes sick leave, insurance, and similar benefits. However, employers who do not provide sick leave or short term disability benefits to workers are not required to provide them to pregnant workers.

*Quid pro quo* sexual harassment involves supervisory personnel seeking sexual favors from employees under them in return for job benefits such as continued employment, promotions, raises, or a favorable performance evaluation. In such a case, when a supervisor's actions affect job benefits, Title VII's prohibition against sex discrimination comes into play, and the employer is liable under this Act.

A second form of sexual harassment is the so-called *hostile working environment harassment.* This a situation where a supervisor's conduct has sexual connotations and has caused anxiety or poisoned the work environment. This type of conduct may include such things as unwelcome flirtations, propositions, or any other abuse of a sexual nature. If this type of conduct causes an employee to quit his or her job, the employer may be liable for any damage caused to the employee.

**The Age Discrimination in Employment Act** (ADEA) prohibits discrimination against men and women over 40 and also prohibits mandatory retirement because of age. There are some exceptions to this mandatory retirement aspect. This Act only covers employers with 20 or more employees. The Older Workers Benefit Protection Act of 1990 (OWBPA) prohibits age discrimination in connection with employee benefits unless the employer can prove that the cost of benefits for older workers is more than for younger workers. Employers commonly require that employees taking early retirement packages waive all claims against their employers, including, any claim they have under ADEA. The OWBPA requires that employees be given a specific period of time to evaluate the package, and also requires employers to pay for eight hours of an attorney's time to aid each employee in this evaluation.

The **Americans with Disabilities Act** (ADA) makes it unlawful for an employer to discriminate against any qualified individual with a disability because of the disability. A qualified individual with a disability is any person who, with or without reasonable accommodation, can perform the essential functions of the job. The ADA applies to virtually every employment practice, from the application procedures for hiring to compensation, training, other terms and conditions of employment, and discharge. The statute defines reasonable accommodation to include physical alteration of existing facilities to make them accessible to people with disabilities, restructuring jobs, allowing part-time or modified working schedules, acquiring or modifying equipment, and hiring qualified readers for the blind or interpreters for the deaf. The ADA defines disability very broadly and includes any person with: (1) a physical or mental impairment which substantially limits one or more of the individual's major life activities; (2) a record of such an impairment; or (3) an individual who is regarded by the employer as having such an impairment. The test is a two-pronged test. First, you must decide whether or not there is a physical or mental impairment. If so, you must decide whether or not it substantially limits a major life function.

# VI. ANTITRUST AND LABOR ISSUES IN SPORTS

The term antitrust is used to describe any contract or conspiracy that illegally restrains trade and promotes anti-competitive behavior. Think of the term *anti-competition* rather than antitrust. The American economy depends upon the laws of supply and demand - the theory of freedom of competition. Congress enacted antitrust laws to prevent anti-competitive behavior in business in order to promote competition and ultimately drive down prices for consumers.

To protect the rights of workers, unions were formed to negotiate employment contracts collectively in order to achieve a collective bargaining agreement (CBA). In the sports industry, the unions that represent the players are called players associations. Labor and antitrust issues are governed primarily by federal statutes.

The Sherman Antitrust Act prohibits monopolies and restraint of trade. For example, several suppliers of widgets get together and agree they will all sell widgets for $1.00 to stores, and no less. This hurts competition. This Act prohibits:

- a conspiracy by two or more persons to unreasonably restrain trade (i.e., to unreasonably limit competition;

- an unlawful monopoly or an attempt to monopolize an industry; and

- price fixing.

The Sherman Act doesn't regulate how big a company may get unless company continues to buy up other companies in such a way as to:

- substantially lessen competition; and

- tend to create a monopoly.

Violations of the Sherman Act may subject the wrongdoer to criminal penalties. Individuals may be fined by the government up to $350,000 per violation while corporations may be fined up to $10 million per violation. The government may also pursue civil damages for violations of the Sherman Act and such damages are automatically trebled (tripled). Additionally, reasonable costs and attorneys fees may be awarded.

The Clayton Act prohibits a corporation from acquiring an interest in the stock or assets of another corporation if doing so substantially lessens competition or may create a monopoly. A Federal Court may enter a divestiture order making the guilty party give up the property it acquired. This Act also allows the government or a private plaintiff to obtain an injunction against anti-competitive behavior. The Norris-LaGuardia Act was passed in 1932 and allows employees to organize as a collective bargaining units. This allows the employer to negotiate a contract that governs all covered employees as one unit.

The National Labor Relations Act was passed in 1935.This Act guarantees employees the right to form a labor union and requires employers to deal with a duly-elected union as the bargaining agent for the employees. The NLRA prohibits employers from interfering with employees and from discriminating against an employee as a result of the employee's union activity. The NLRA requires good faith bargaining. However, it does not compel either party to agree to a proposal or require the making of a concession.

The National Labor Relations Board (NLRB) is a independent federal agency which administers and enforces the NLRA. Its two primary functions are to conduct elections in which employees decide whether a labor organization is to represent them, and to investigate and remedy unlawful labor practices committed by a labor union or employer. The NLRB investigates charges of unfair labor practices and can either dismiss the charge or pursue it further by issuing a complaint against the union or employer. The complaint is heard by an administrative law judge who sends a recommended decision to the NLRB, which issues a final decision and order. Anyone who wants to appeal the NLRB order may petition to a U. S. Court of Appeals.

*Monopolizing* is prohibited by section 2 of the Sherman Act. However, some monopolies are permitted. For example, newspapers can be a monopoly in a town that can't support but one. Also, a monopoly which is the result of superior skill, foresight, and industry will be permitted. West Publishing Company had a monopoly for a long time regarding the publishing of legal opinions. They were the first publishing company, to my knowledge, to publish state and federal appellate court opinions on a large scale basis. They are still the best in the business, although they do have a little competition. The Internet is eventually going to hurt their business, since court opinions are now being put on the web.

The elements of monopolization are twofold:

- possession of monopoly power in a relevant market; and

- willfully acquiring or maintaining that power.

When a court uses what is called the *per se* rule analysis, any labor practices that are inherently unreasonable restraints of trade will be invalidated. In *Northern Pacific Railway Co. v. United States,* 356 U.S. 1 (1958), the United States Supreme Court stated that certain agreements or practices, because of their adverse effect on competition, are conclusively presumed to be unreasonable and therefore illegal. For example, price fixing is a per se violation of antitrust laws. Price fixing is anticompetitive and hurts consumers. Under the rule of reason analysis, a court must examine the labor practice at issue and determine whether it is reasonable or unreasonable. Some restraints are necessary as a legitimate business practice.

Congress favors the process of collective bargaining rather than having to ask the courts to intervene in labor disputes. In *Brown v. Pro Football, Inc.,* 518 U.S 231 (1996),the U.S. Supreme Court made its position clear that courts should become less involved in disputes that arise from the collective bargaining process. The NLRA gives workers the right to strike if a CBA cannot be reached. Before a strike can occur, the union members must vote and there must be a majority in favor of a strike. The union must then give the employer 60 days notice (cooling off period).

Also, if a CBA cannot be reached the employer may prevent its own employees from working. This is called a *lockout.*

Baseball, football, basketball, and hockey have all had legal battles involving the application of the antitrust laws. Baseball has held a unique exemption from antitrust laws in accordance with the interpretation of the Supreme Court in *Federal Baseball Club of Baltimore, Inc. v. National League of Professional Baseball Clubs* (1922). The Court held that antitrust laws do not apply to professional baseball. Professional baseball had a reserve system in which once a player signed with a team, he became the property of that team only until he retired from the team or the team no longer wanted him. Major League Baseball (MLB) has had eight work stoppages since 1972, with player strikes or owner lockouts causing the cancellation or postponement of games in 1972, 1981, 1985, and 1994, as well as spring training cancellation in 1990. The MLBPA was formed in 1954, and MLB had its first collective bargaining agreement in 1968. To date, the baseball players association has won virtually all of the labor disputes. This accounts for baseball players having the highest salaries among the four major sports leagues.

In one of the most controversial opinions of the U.S. Supreme Court, baseball was held to not involve interstate commerce (as required by the Sherman Act) in *Federal Baseball Club of Baltimore, Inc. v. National League of Professional Baseball Clubs*. Even though players traveled across state lines, Justice Oliver Wendell Holmes held that it was only incidental to the game; baseball was purely a state affair and held to remain exempt from antitrust laws. Baseball used the reserve clause, which precluded players from jumping to another baseball league, the Federal Baseball League. Therefore, since the court held that antitrust laws did not apply to baseball, baseball's reserve clause was acceptable.

Curtis Flood was a Major League Baseball player, primarily a center fielder, for the Cincinnati Reds (1956-

1957) and the St. Louis Cardinals from 1958-1971). He was a three-time All-Star and seven-time Gold Glove Award winner. He hit .300 or better six times during his 15-year major league career and had a lifetime batting average of .293. As a fielder, Flood was once went 226 consecutive games without making an error.

Curt Flood's greatest years were with the Cardinals. He had a league-leading 211 hits for the Cardinals in 1964, and played on his first of two World Series championship teams that season. Though not usually thought of as a power hitter, Flood had 11 home runs and 83 runs-batted-in in 1966. In 1967, he hit for a .335 average in helping the Cardinals to another World Series championship. However, Curt Flood will probably be best remembered for challenging Major League Baseball's reserve clause. He maintained that it was unfair in that it kept players beholden to the team with whom they originally signed for life, even though players had satisfied the terms and conditions of those contracts. In 1969, the St. Louis Cardinals traded Flood to the Philadelphia Phillies. However, Flood refused to report to the Phillies, citing the team's poor record and the fact that they played in dilapidated Connie Mack Stadium. Flood also believed, that the Phillies had racist fans at that time. Curt Flood forfeited a relatively lucrative $100,000 contract by his refusal to be traded to the Phillies.

In a letter to Major League Baseball commissioner Bowie Kuhn, Curt Flood demanded that the commissioner declare him a free agent. "After twelve years in the Major Leagues, I do not feel I am a piece of property to be bought and sold irrespective of my wishes. I believe that any system which produces that result violates my basic rights as a citizen and is inconsistent with the laws of the

United States and of the sovereign States. It is my desire to play baseball in 1970, and I am capable of playing. I have received a contract offer from the Philadelphia Club, but I believe I have the right to consider offers from other clubs before making any decisions. I, therefore, request that you make known to all Major League Clubs my feelings in this matter, and advise them of my availability for the 1970 season."

Commissioner Bowie Kuhn denied his request, citing the propriety of the reserve clause. In response, Curt Flood filed a lawsuit against Kuhn and Major League Baseball on January 16, 1970, alleging that Major League Baseball had violated federal antitrust laws. Even though Flood was making $90,000 at the time, he likened the reserve clause to slavery. Arguably, it was a controversial analogy, even among those who opposed the reserve clause. The case, *Flood v. Kuhn,* (407 U.S. 258,) eventually went to the Supreme Court. Flood's attorney, former Supreme Court Justice Arthur Goldberg, asserted that the reserve clause depressed wages and limited players to one team for life. Ultimately, the Supreme Court, acting on stare decisis "to stand by things decided", ruled 5-3 in favor of Major League Baseball, upholding the 1922 ruling in the case of *Federal Baseball Club v. National League.*

Curt Flood sat out the entire 1970 season. Curt Flood played with the Washington Senators in 1971. His short tenure with the Senators was a failure. Pitcher Bob Gibson wrote that Flood once returned to his locker to find a funeral wreath on it. Despite manager Ted Williams' vote of confidence, Flood retired after only playing in 13 games and batting .200.

Ironically, even though Curt Flood lost the lawsuit, the

reserve clause was struck down in 1975. Arbitrator Peter Seitz ruled that since pitchers Andy Messersmith and Dave McNally played for one season without a contract, they could become free agents. This decision essentially dismantled the reserve clause and opened up the door to free agency. Curt Flood died of throat cancer in Los Angeles, California at age 59.

In *Mackey v. NFL, 543 F.2d 606* (8th Cir. 1976), John Mackey, a tight end for the Baltimore Colts challenges the *Rozelle Rule*. This rule stated that when a player's contract expired and he signed with a new team, that team had to adequately compensate the former team. The Court ultimately held that the Roselle Rule was an unreasonable restraint of trade. In Mackey, the Eighth Circuit set forth a three-prong test for assessing the applicability of the exemption, which several other circuits have since adopted. The three-prong Mackey test, under which the exemption is appropriate only when:

- The agreement sought to be exempted concerns a mandatory subject of collective bargaining;

- The restraint on trade primarily affects only the parties to the collective bargaining relationship; and

- The agreement is the product of bona fide arm's-length bargaining.

The players' strike in 1987 became one of the most publicized labor disputes in history. On September 22, 1987, the NFL players went on strike after unsuccessful negotiations with the owners about, primarily, free agency. During the 1987 strike, NFL owners hired replacement players (referred by some as scabs) to continue the season. This fielding of replacement players in 1987 has been referred to as the darkest period of labor relations in professional football. Some NFL players crossed the picket lines to play. Television networks broadcast the scab games using replacement players. This pitted players against players.

After the 1987 strike demonstrated that traditional collective bargaining practices would probably not obtain a contract with the owners, the NFLPA turned to the courts. For five years after the 1987 strike, NFL players worked with no contract in place, and both sides spent more time in the courtroom than at the collective bargaining table. A contract was finally reached between the owners and players union. This contract, especially its salary cap feature, has caused a great deal of pressure on other sports to follow suit.

Professional basketball players organized their union, the NBA Players Union, in the 1950s, about the same time baseball players organized collectively. Now known as the NBA Players Association (NBPA), the NBPA has been successful in its advocacy efforts on behalf of professional basketball players and has never participated in a labor strike against NBA team owners.

In *Wood v. National Basketball Association*, 809 F.2d. 954 (2d. Cir. 1987), the U.S. Court of Appeals for the Second Circuit dismissed a player's antitrust claim challenging certain provisions of a CBA between the NBA and NBPA. Wood, a college senior, challenged the NBA salary cap, the NBA draft, and restricted free agency. The court found that the challenged provisions were mandatory subjects of collective bargaining and therefore were protected by the non-statutory labor exemption. This exemption describes the court's holdings that any CBA will receive protection from federal antitrust laws.

Hockey has had the fewest antitrust challenges of the four major sports. The NHLPA's existence began in 1967. Still, a few issues have required judicial intervention. Similar to professional basketball in recent years, hockey has enjoyed a surge in popularity and prosperity as the fan base has increased, merchandising revenues have increased, television revenues have increased, and teams have moved to newer and more modern arenas across the country. It is likely that as hockey continues to expand teams in the United States and Canada, antitrust laws will likely be called upon to resolve a dispute. There have been several challenges to the market power of professional sports leagues by rival, newly formed upstart leagues. Professional football has had several challenges to its domination of the American marketplace. While newer leagues attempt to form a fan base and gain much needed television contracts for their survival, allegations of antitrust violations are common, particularly if the newer league ultimately folds.

In *American Football League v. National Football League,* 323 F.2d 124 (4th Cir. 1963), the AFL claimed that the NFL was a monopoly and sued alleging antitrust violations. However, the Fourth Circuit Court held that the NFL was a natural monopoly and did not violate antitrust laws.

Amateur sports in America do not have nearly as many legal challenges involving antitrust laws. Courts seem to have afforded amateur athletic organizations more latitude and less scrutiny. Several cases involving antitrust analysis in the amateur sports context have offered some guidance and certainty as to how antitrust laws should apply in the amateur sports context. For example, in *NCAA v. Bd. of Regents of Univ. of Okla.,* 468 U.S. 85 (1984), the NCAA's television broadcast plan was held to be anti-competitive and in violation of the Sherman Act.

In *Law v. NCAA,* 134 F.3d 1010 (10th Cir. 1998), the NCAA was again found to be in violation of federal antitrust laws when it implemented the REC (restricted-earnings coaches) Rule. This rule limited the compensation of assistant coaches in all NCAA Division I sports to a mere $12,000 per year plus a possible $4,000 in the summer months. The rule was enacted as a cost-cutting measure among NCAA institutions that claimed that it also provided for a more competitive balance among member institutions. A group of coaches challenged the rule as being in violation of Section 1 of the Sherman Act, and the federal court found that the rule was anticompetitive and an unlawful restraint of trade. The NCAA was ordered to pay over $22 million in damages that was trebled to $67 million. The case finally settled for $54.5 million.

# VII.  INTELLECTUAL PROPERTY RIGHTS

## Trademarks and Service Marks

A "trademark" is a word, design or combination used by an individual or a business to identify its goods or services. In some cases a trademark can also be a sensory mark--a sound, a color or a smell. While marks identifying services rather than goods are technically referred to a "service marks" we will use the term *trademarks* to include service marks. Trademarks protect names used to identify goods (or services) and their source of origin. The law protects trademarks in part because trademarked items tend to carry with them certain quality assurances - one would expect an automobile carrying the Rolls Royce trademark to be far superior to most other automobiles. You may use any kind of name or symbol as a trademark to identify your product.

A mark is any word, name, symbol, or design that identifies a product or service. A trademark identifies a product (for example, *Coca-Cola*). A service mark identifies a service (for example, *Holiday Inn*). A mark may be registered with the United States Patent and Trademark Office (USPTO) if the mark distinguishes a person's product or service from products or services of competitors. Registration of a mark on the Principal Register of the USPTO entitles a person the exclusive use of the mark. Registration can also be accomplished with a State (usually with the Secretary of State of a particular state). However, State registration does not provide as much protection as Federal registration. Before a mark can be registered, it must be used by the United States Patent and Trademark Office and it must distinguish goods or services from others. The owner of a mark cannot register it with the United States Patent and Trademark Office unless the mark is used in interstate commerce.

Generic terms that merely describe a class of products cannot be registered. For example, the term *motor oil* or the word *airline* would not be accepted for registration. Descriptive or geographical terms cannot be registered unless they have acquired a secondary meaning. A mark acquires a secondary meaning when, through long usage, the public identifies the mark with a particular product. For example, Best Western Motels involves a mark which has a secondary meaning.

One can be an owner of a trademark or service mark, whether or not it is registered. This is common law protection. Registration is proof of ownership and makes ownership rights easier to enforce. The basic question in lawsuits over marks is whether or not the general public is likely to be confused as to the origin of the service or product. If the owner of a mark permits widespread use of the mark to describe a general class of products, the exclusive right to the mark may be lost. Two examples are *cellophane* and *aspirin.*

**Trade dress** is the total appearance of a product, including its packaging, label, shape, and size. Trade dress may also include physical structures associated with a particular product or service, such as the "golden arches" of McDonald's. Trade dress may qualify as a protected trademark or service mark if it is distinctive and identifies the source of a specific product or service.

**Copyrights**

A copyright offers protection for original works of authorship. Copyright protection affords the author of a copyrighted work with specific rights that the author can give or sell to others or keep for himself. The concept of copyright protection in the United States is set forth in the original U.S. Constitution which allows Congress to pass laws that promote and encourage the process of the useful arts.

The word *copyright* can be defined as a property right in an original work of authorship (such as a literary, musical, artistic, photographic, or film work) fixed in any tangible medium of expression, giving the holder the exclusive right to reproduce, adapt, distribute, perform, and display the work. Copyright protection may be received regarding a wide range of creative, intellectual, or artistic forms or works. These include poems, plays, and other literary works, movies, choreographic works (dances, ballets, etc.), musical compositions, audio recordings, paintings, drawings, sculptures, photographs, radio and television broadcasts. The creator of the work has a limited monopoly on the work and can, with some exceptions, prohibit others from copying or displaying the work. The United States copyright law is contained in Chapters 1 through 8 and 10 through 12 of Title 17 of the United States Code.

Works published after 1922, but before 1978 are protected for 95 years from the date of publication. If the work was created, but not published, before 1978, the copyright lasts for the life of the author plus 70 years. However, even if the author died over 70 years ago, the copyright in an unpublished work lasts until December 31, 2002. And if such a work is published before December 31, 2002, the copyright will last until December 31, 2047. All works published in the United States before 1923 are in the public domain.

The term *public domain* refers to creative materials that are not protected by intellectual property laws such as copyright, trademark or patent laws. The public owns these works, not an individual author or artist. Anyone can use a public domain work without obtaining permission, but no one can ever own it. Once a copyright expires, it is in the public domain and no longer has protection. Works created by the federal government are also in the public domain.

A copyright is obtained simply by creating the work. It comes into existence automatically on the date it is created. However, in order to get federal protection of a copyright, the creator of the work has to file two copies of the work with the Copyright Office in Washington, D.C.

Copyright law is designed to create an incentive for creativity by allowing the author to profit from his work. The Act tries to balance this need to protect the author with the public's need for free and open discussion. A copyright owner has the exclusive right to:

- Reproduce the work;

- Prepare derivative works, such as a script from the original work (e.g., movie script for Book *The Rainmaker*);

- Distribute copies or recordings of the work; and

- Publicly display the work in the case of paintings, sculptures and photographs.

The Copyright Act contains several exemptions that allow a person or institution to use or copy a copyrighted work without the owner's permission. Three commonly used exemptions are:

- the *fair use doctrine* which allows copying for such purposes such as teaching;

- the right of libraries to make limited copies; and

- certain performances and displays for teaching or religious purposes.

The fair use doctrine allows reasonable use of copyrighted works (without requiring the author's permission) for teaching, research, and news reporting. The Federal Act states: "[T]he fair use of a copyrighted work, including such use by reproduction in copies . . . for purposes such as criticism, comment, news reporting, teaching (including multiple copies for classroom use), scholarship, or research, is not an infringement of copyright."

There are four important factors that must be looked at when determining whether or not the fair use doctrine applies:

- the purpose of the use, including whether such use is of a commercial nature or is for nonprofit educational purposes;

- the nature of the copyrighted work;

- the amount of the portion used in relation to the copyrighted work as a whole; and

- the effect of the use on the potential market for or value of the copyrighted work.

If a work is a *work made for hire,* this means that a person was hired specifically to create the copyrighted work. The employer of the creator of the work can register the copyright and is entitled to protection.

## Patents

A patent is a grant of a property right by the Government to an inventor. The United States Constitution gives Congress the right to provide for patent protection in legislation in order to encourage useful inventions. The patent itself provides a detailed description of the invention, and how it is used or how to make it. Thus, if you obtain a patent you cannot keep the matter secret, which is the province of trade secrets laws. A patent enables the owner to exclude others from making, using or selling the invention for the life of the patent. Federal statutes give an inventor the exclusive right to use, sell, and market his invention.

## Trade Secrets

A formula, process, or information that is secret, and gives its owner a business advantage may be protected under State laws concerning trade secrets. Trade secrets, basically, are any formula, device, or information that is used in a business, and is of such a nature that it gives the owner an advantage over competitors who do not have the information. Customer lists may be protected unless they can be easily developed from public information. Trade secrets are protected under State law rather than Federal law. This protection may be by virtue of common law or statutory law, such as the Uniform Trade Secrets Act.

When a trade secret is made public, it loses its protection as a trade secret unless it is disclosed in a restrictive manner to persons who know of its confidential nature.

## Remedies for Violation of Property Rights

When property is harmed, taken, or destroyed, the most common remedy is an action for monetary damages. The property itself may be recovered if unlawfully taken. Wrongful use of a copyright, trademark, service mark, or patent can result in injunctive action, as well as a suit for damages. If an infringement is intentional, profits resulting from the infringement may also be obtained.

Infringement of a trademark or service mark occurs when a person uses or copies the trademark or service mark of another person without the person's permission (e.g., putting *Nike* label on shoes and selling them).

**Ambush Marketing** is a phrase that describes the actions of companies that seek to associate themselves with a sponsored event such as the Olympic Games or the Super Bowl without paying the requisite fee as official sponsors do. The ambush consists of giving the impression to consumers that the organization/company is actually a sponsor or is somehow affiliated with the event when in fact it is not.[29]

Examples include:

- In the 1996 Atlanta Olympics, sprinter Linford Christie wore contact lenses embossed with the *Puma* logo at the press conference preceding the 100 meters final, despite *Reebok* being the official sponsor.

- In the 1996 Atlanta Olympics, *Messages On Hold* strategically infiltrated a banner within the camera frame as U.S. runner Jon Drummond prepared for the opening leg of 4x100 relay final. The moment was broadcast live across the world.

- In the 1996 Cricket World Cup, Pepsi ran a series of

---

[29] *Sports Law* at p. 252 by Adam Epstein, Delmar Leaning (2003)

advertisements entitled *Nothing Official About It,* thus targeting the official sponsor *Coca Cola.*

- In the 1998 World Cup, Nike sponsored a number of teams competing in the Cup despite Adidas being the official sponsor.

- In the 2000 Sydney Olympics, Qantas Airlines' slogan *The Spirit of Australia* sounded strikingly similar to the Games' slogan *Share the Spirit.* despite Ansett Air being the official sponsor.

- In the 2003 Cricket World Cup, Indian players threatened to strike over concerns that the anti-ambush marketing rules were too strict. Of particular concern was the length of time before and after the cup that players were not allowed to endorse a rival to one of the official sponsors. Players argued that if they had pre-existing contracts that they would be in breach of them if they were to accept the ICC's rules.

- In the 2006 FIFA World Cup, fans of the Netherlands were made to remove Bavaria Brewery's *Leeuwenhosen* because Budweiser was the official beer sponsor.

- In the 2008 Beijing Olympics; millions of people were tuned into the Opening Ceremonies and saw Li Ning, a former Olympic gymnast for China, light the torch. However, many viewers later learned that Li Ning also owns a shoe company with the same name, *Li Ning,* a direct rival of Adidas and quite famous in China, but not an official Olympic sponsor.[30]

---

[30] *Id*

# VIII.  TITLE IX AND OTHER WOMEN'S ISSUES

Title IX of the Education Amendments of 1972 is a federal law prohibiting gender discrimination in athletic programs at institutions that receive federal funds. What happens to a college that is cut off from federal funds?

Title IX has been a controversial law involving amateur sports. Since it was enacted, the number and quality of female high school and college athletes have increased tremendously as a direct result of this federal law. In October of 2000, a federal jury ruled that Duke discriminated against female place kicker Heather Sue Mercer and awarded her $2 million in punitive damages. She was an all-state kicker at Yorktown Heights High School in Yorktown Heights, New York. She enrolled at Duke University in the fall of 1994 and, upon enrolling, tried out for the football team as a walk-on kicker. She initially did not make the team and instead served as a manager for the football team during the 1994 season. In the spring of 1995, she participated in conditioning drills with the football team and was selected by the seniors on the team to participate in the Blue-White Game, an intrasquad scrimmage played each spring. In the game, Mercer kicked a 28-yard game-winning field goal, giving the Blue team a, 24-22, victory. Soon after the game, Duke head football coach Fred Goldsmith told the news media that Mercer was on the Duke football team. Shortly thereafter, assistant football coach Fred Chatham, Duke's kicking coach, personally told Mercer that she had made the team. Mike Cragg, Duke's sports information director, also asked Mercer to participate in a number of interviews with newspaper, radio, and television reporters. Mercer did not play in any games during the 1995 season, but she regularly attended practices. She was officially listed as a member of the Duke football team on the roster filed with the NCAA and she was pictured in the Duke football yearbook. Despite being officially listed as a member of the team, she was not allowed to dress for games or sit on the sidelines during games. In the spring of 1996, she again participated in conditioning drills with the football team.

It was during this latter period that Mercer alleged that she was subject to discriminatory treatment by Duke. Specifically, she claimed that Goldsmith did not permit her to attend summer camp, refused to allow her to dress for games or sit on the sidelines during games, and gave her fewer opportunities to participate in practices than other walk-on kickers. She also claimed that Goldsmith made a number of offensive comments to her, such as wondering why she did not prefer to participate in beauty pageants rather than football and suggesting that she sit in the stands with her boyfriend rather than on the sideline.

At the beginning of the 1996 season, Goldsmith informed Mercer that she had been dropped from the team. Mercer claims that Goldsmith's decision to drop her from the team was based on her sex since Goldsmith allowed other, less qualified walk-on kickers to remain on the team.

Mercer filed suit against Duke in 1997, claiming Duke football coaches cut her from the football team because she is a woman and treated her differently from male players; thus, the university violated Title IX of the Education Amendments Act of 1972 prohibiting gender discrimination. Under Title IX, Duke was not required to permit her to try out for a contact sport like football, but if she was permitted to try by the football coach, she needed to be treated the same as any other student athlete who tried out. Duke argued that Mercer was cut from the team based on her abilities. Former head coach Fred Goldsmith testified that Mercer's lack of speed, size and leg strength kept her from being considered for play.

What is the purpose of college athletics? Title IX is often referred to as the gender equity statute. Some say Title IX as the necessary equivalent of affirmative action for women in sports. Others argue that Title IX is an unjust quota system that punishes male athletes and programs.

## Born from the Civil Rights Movement

Title IX actually evolved from and amended Title VII of the Civil Rights Act of 1964. Title VII provides that an employer may not discriminate on the basis of race, color, religion, sex, or national origin. Title IX extends that same philosophy to any program that receives funding from the federal government: It must not discriminate on the basis of gender when it comes to applying the funds to sports programs. Title IX states:

*No person in the United States shall, on the basis of sex, be excluded from participation in, be denied the benefits of, or be subjected to discrimination under any education program or activity receiving Federal financial assistance.*

As a result of this legislation, women have directly benefitted from the creation of new programs and new opportunities to compete at the highest amateur level.

Additionally, professional leagues in several sports such as the Women's National Basketball Association (WNBA) and the women's United Soccer Association (WUSA) continue to expand and create even more possibilities for women as professional athletes.

**College Sports**

Title IX has led to an increase in female participation in sports at both the high school and collegiate levels. Collegiate athletic departments and universities that do not comply with Title IX may be subject to severe penalties by the federal government, including termination of federal funds. However, no such penalty has ever been handed down.[31]

Pursuant to Title VI of the 1964 Civil Rights Act, each federal department and agency that disburses federal funds is required to establish procedures for determining that grant recipients do not discriminate. In 1979, Congress split the Department of Health, Education and Welfare (HEW) into the Department of Health and Human Services (HHS) and the Department of Education (DOE), transferring all the education and enforcement functions of the former HEW to the DOE. Title IX administration also was assigned to US Department of Education's Office of Civil Rights (OCR). The DOE's office is headed by the Assistant Secretary of Education for Civil Rights.

In 1979, the Office of Civil Rights (OCR) published regulations regarding how Title IX should be interpreted. These regulations compared areas of financial assistance and other funding categories for both men's and women's sports programs. Based on the OCR's interpretation, these

---

[31] *Sports Law* at p.104 by Adam Epstein, Delmar Leaning (2003)

factors must be taken into account when comparing Title IX compliance between men's and women's programs:

(1) equipment and supplies;

(2) scheduling of games and practice time;

(3) travel and per diem allowances;

(4) tutoring;

(5) coaching;

(6) locker rooms, practice, and competitive facilities;

(7) medical and training facilities and services;

(8) housing and dining facilities and services;

(9) publicity;

(10) support services; and

(11) recruitment of student-athletes (e.g., budget).

Title IX ultimately analyzes whether or not money is being allocated equitably between men's and women's programs based on the number of students attending such schools. The key component in a Title IX cases is whether the institution developed a plan and carried out its mission to expand and accommodate the interests of female student-athletes, coaches, and administrators. Developing a plan is not enough: Carrying out its mission is the key.

**Title IX Criticism**

The fundamental purpose of Title IX is designed to help prevent gender discrimination. However the practical application of this law has generated violent debate. Many opponents of Title IX argue that the law has turned into a quota system and has contributed to the systematic destruction of male sports programs throughout the United

States. Many male swimming, wrestling, football, water polo, baseball, and other programs have been eliminated in the name of Title IX compliance. Almost all of the programs that are eliminated are classified as *non-revenue producing* sports according to the NCAA. Supporters of the law argue that Title IX continues to benefit women socially, economically, and even emotionally. Much of the criticism of this law involves the interpretation of how it is applied.[32]

**Grove City College v. Bell**

In 1984 the U.S. Supreme Court granted a major victory for many collegiate athletic departments by holding that Title IX did not apply to collegiate athletic programs in the case of *Grove City College v. Bell*, 465 U.S. 555 (1984). The Supreme Court held that Title IX only applied to the specific programs that received federal (taxpayer) funds and not the athletic departments themselves (none of whom received direct federal financial assistance). This victory, however was short lived. In 1988 Congress enacted the Civil Rights Restoration Act and, in effect, reversed this decision. Title IX therefore mandates that college athletic departments are no longer immune from its interpretation, and are forced to comply with its regulations.

**Title IX Tests**

In order to comply with Title IX according to the U.S. Department of Education, a school must meet one of three tests. Currently the OCR oversees compliance in this area and in 1996 offered a clarification of what Title IX compliance really means. If a school passes any one of the three tests, then theoretically there is compliance.

---

[32] *Id* at p. 105

Passing these tests is often referred to as the *safe harbor* interpretations of the statute.

## Test 1: Substantial Proportionality

*Question:* Is an institution providing participation opportunities for women and men that are substantially proportionate to their respective rates of enrollment as full-lime undergraduate students?

The *substantial proportionality* test is the one that is most often used by plaintiffs and courts to determine whether an institution is in compliance with Title IX. It is usually the easiest method to assess compliance because it is based on numbers. If, for example, 50 percent of women are full-time undergraduates enrolled at a particular college, then 50 percent of the participants in sports programs there must be women. There has been considerable debate as to what the substantial proportionality test means in terms of a specific statistical ratio that athletic departments must adhere to in order to be in compliance.[33] While ideally the ratio would be 50 - 50, such a ratio has been difficult for athletic departments and universities to achieve. What, then, is substantial proportionality? In *Roberts v. Colorado State Board of Agriculture,* 998 F.2d 824 (10th Cir. 1993), the court held that a disparity of 10.5% did not meet the substantial proportionality test.

## Test 2: History of Expansion of Women's Programs

*Question:* Has an institution demonstrated a history and continuing practice of program expansion for the underrepresented sex?

If an institution can demonstrate a history of expansion of

---

[33] *Id* at p. 106

women's sports programs, then the institution is likely to survive a claim against it charging noncompliance. However, virtually no court and no institution was able to address this issue successfully until Syracuse University demonstrated compliance in this area with a potentially major legal victory in 1999.[34]

## Test 3: Full and Effective Accommodation of Women's Interests

*Question:* Has an institution fully and effectively accommodated the interests and abilities of the under represented sex?

Proving that women (or men) are having their interests effectively accommodated is virtually impossible. Recommendations have included conducting on-campus surveys.

## Evolution of Title IX

The interpretation of Title IX and its effect on student-athletes and institutions has had its greatest impact in the legal system from cases brought by individuals suing their own institution for failing to comply with the federal law. The case of *Franklin v. Gwinnett County Public Schools,* 503 U.S. 60 (1992) allows for individuals to sue and recover monetary damages for violations of Title IX.[35]

## Cohen v. Brown University, 101 F.3d 155 (1st Cir. 1996)

This case is generally regarded as the most influential Title IX case ever to be decided. In 1991, Brown University announced that it was going to eliminate four sports: women's volleyball, women's gymnastics, men's golf, and

---

[34] *Id* at p. 107
[35] *Id*

men's water polo. Brown University said the teams could still compete as club sports, but it was not going to provide university funding due to financial pitfalls. At that time, Brown's student body was comprised of 52 percent male and 48 percent female students, though 63 percent of its student-athletes were male. Amy Cohen, a member of the gymnastics team, sued Brown, and the trial court held that Brown failed all three tests under Title IX. An appeal was filed with the United States Supreme Court, which subsequently declined to hear the case.[36]

## NCAA V. Smith, 525 U.S. 459 (1999)

In this case, Smith was a female volleyball player who attempted to play at two universities in violation of NCAA transfer and eligibility rules. The NCAA did not allow her to play, and Smith sued the NCAA alleging violations of Title IX. Even though the NCAA does not receive federal funds directly, its member institutions do and they pay money to be members of the NCAA. The Supreme Court held that dues payments do not raise the NCAA to the level of a *covered program or activity* under Title IX, even though its member institutions must still comply. Therefore, the NCAA as an organization appears to be safe from Title IX attacks for the time being.[37]

Television and sports reporters across America extolled the 1996 Summer Olympics as the Olympics in which American women dominated. The American women's gymnastics, soccer and softball teams all won gold medals. Amy Van Dyken won four gold medals in swimming, the most gold medals any American woman has won at an Olympics, and the volleyball team excited

---

[36] *Id*
[37] *Id* at p. 113

new interest in that game. Today, one can't help but notice that the sports page regularly carries news about national and local women's sports. Television stations post scores for girls' teams as well as those for the boys. However, it wasn't always that way.

Women and girls have not always enjoyed the opportunity to participate in sports teams while attending school. In an attempt to assure equality between the sexes, Congress passed Title IX of the Education Amendment in 1972. The major provision of Title IX was that no person would be denied access to participation based on sex in any educational program receiving federal financial assistance. Most schools, even some private ones, receive federal assistance, so that meant all physical education and sports programs had to comply.

Twenty-five years later, the effects of this law are emerging. Some progress toward equality in participation has been made, particularly in the area of intercollegiate sports opportunities for women and more equity in school sports budgets. But not everyone supports the law. It has taken lawsuits against violations of the law across the country to make women's sports visible throughout the U.S.

A landmark lawsuit was filed against Brown University in April 1993 by nine female athletes for failure to provide sufficient opportunities for sports participation. A lawyer for the school argued that there was more interest in men's sports than women's. He also argued that there was more participation from men than women in sports. The court ruled that the University reinstate the women's gymnastic and volleyball teams to full varsity status. Brown University appealed, which resulted in the first appellate court decision to apply federal sex-discrimination laws to college sports. Judge Bruce Selya upheld the lower court's decision ordering Brown University to reinstate the teams. In April 1997, the case went to the U.S. Supreme Court which upheld the appellate court's decision and rejected Brown's position that it was not discriminating, but merely reflecting the difference in interest in men's and women's sports. This ruling will influence schools all over the country that have either ignored or defied Title IX guidelines.

Title IX complaints have also been filed at the high school level. Nancy Williams, New Jersey Shore Regional High School girls' softball and field hockey coach, filed a complaint in August of 1996. Her complaint was against the West Long Branch Board of Education for voting not to rehire her despite having a winning record. Williams also complained about the inequalities in the girls' sports programs at the school. Female athletes were not provided with the same number of coaches, equipment and locker rooms that the boys had. The school did not videotape girls' sports, provide cheerleaders, concession stands or bands for their events. These complaints caused the school to be investigated by the federal Department of Education. The school was found guilty of discriminating against female athletes, and a settlement was reached with the Department of Education to give girls' sports more attention, support and funding. Salaries of the coaches for the girls were also to become equal to those of the boys' coaches.

Since the passage of Title IX in 1972, participation in college women's sports has increased. According to NCAA statistics, the total number of female athletes increased by 25 percent in the first 20 years, and between 1992 and 1996, at least 800 women's teams have been added at the collegiate level. Locally, women are enjoying participating in teams that did not exist in the 1970s. The University of Texas at El Paso offers women's teams in basketball, volleyball, track and field, tennis, soccer and golf, with swimming and softball to be added soon.

Every district in the El Paso area supports women's teams in high school volleyball, basketball, tennis, golf, and track. Swimming and softball are available in the El Paso, Ysleta and Socorro districts. Ysleta also supports a women's gymnastics team.

El Paso Community College has recently added sports to its programs. The men's baseball team was quickly followed by a women's softball team. Celina Estrada, the starting shortstop, said in an interview, "College softball is different from high school softball because it is more competitive." And player Edna Garcia adds, "All they [women] need is dedication and love for the sport."

Although women have welcomed the new opportunities to participate in sports, not everyone is happy. Finding the funding for each of the sports for both boys and girls is not easy. Budgets may have to be cut from one area in order to accommodate another. Football has always been the number one moneymaking sport at colleges and universities. Coaches and administrators argue that taking money away would be crippling to the sport. "You can't bite the hand that feeds you," says Michigan State football coach George Perles.

But colleges are finding money to support women's sports by reducing spending in other men's sports, sometimes eliminating them outright. For instance, in light of the recent U.S. Supreme Court ruling, Michigan State will reduce funding for men's fencing and lacrosse in order to add women's rowing and remain in compliance with Title IX. Since 1972, 256 colleges have dropped wrestling.

Schools would rather do away with low-profile sports than interfere with football. Other men's sports being cut include field hockey and water polo. Just as racial attitudes could not be changed by legislation overnight, neither can discriminatory attitudes toward women in sports be reversed quickly. Attitude changes have been slow in coming. At the beginning of the 20th century, sports were considered for men only, and women were called "unnatural" and "unladylike" if they showed the slightest interest in participating in sports. According to the New York Times, running was the first sport for women that society finally accepted. But women were not considered physiologically capable of long-distance running. Some believed that a woman who attempted this would not be able to bear children because her uterus might fall out, that she could grow a mustache or that she wanted to be a man. Today these beliefs appear ridiculous, and this generation's women are stronger and healthier than ever before. Women from all ethnic backgrounds are succeeding in high school, college, professional and Olympic sports.

**Men and Title IX**

Male sports programs have become victims of Title IX with regard to interpretation of Title IX compliance that has focused on substantial proportionality. Numerous colleges have cut programs that served the interest of male student-athletes. Historically, sports programs for male student-athletes have been larger and better funded than female programs. Are males, therefore, unable to claim reverse discrimination under a Title IX analysis? Probably not. Title IX is gender neutral and applies equally to men and women - at least in theory. A few cases have been brought by male administrators and student-athletes on the basis of allegations of reverse discrimination, but they have usually failed under a Title IX analysis.[38]

## Men's Programs Funding Women's Programs

Men's sports often fund women's sports for survival. This is the reason for much of the debate that rages among opponents to Title IX. They argue that *revenue sports* such as football and men's basketball serve as the cash cow for women's sports nationwide. Is it fair, then, that men's programs should continue to be cut in order to comply with Title IX while women's programs continue to receive aid from men's programs for their very existence? Though such an argument seems to have merit, it is not usually considered a valid one under a Title IX analysis.[39]

## Contact Sports Exception

A recent interpretation of Title IX involves the issue of contact sports. Prior decisions had mandated that schools must provide women with the opportunity to compete on male teams when no women's team existed. Title IX regulations governing athletics now exempt contact sports to some extent. Sports in this category include boxing. wrestling, rugby, ice hockey, football, basketball, and other sports in which the major activity involves bodily contact. The effect is that women appear to be excluded from participation on all male teams. Once a woman is allowed to compete in that particular sport, the woman may not be treated differently than any other person on account of her gender.[40]

---

[38] *Id* at p. 114
[39] *Id*
[40] *Id*

**Football**

There are no women's football programs at the intercollegiate level. How does an institution comply with the numerical equivalency requirement in terms of participation and the financial responsibilities associated with Title IX when 85 scholarships may be awarded by any Division I program for which there is no women's sports equivalent? Such inequity has been dealt with by athletic departments by eliminating men's programs and adding women's programs. This balances the numerical imbalance in terms of proportionality. Unfortunately, male athletes in sports such as swimming, wrestling, tennis, and baseball have suffered at the expense of compliance-based numbers and percentages. Many individuals hope that subsequent interpretations of Title IX will exclude the sport of football.[41]

**Men's Programs Cut Due to Title IX**

Since Title IX has been enforced, numerous men's programs have been eliminated from athletic departments. Some of these programs, such as UCLA's men's swimming program, provided some of the finest amateur, Olympic, and professional athletes in our country's history. Male victims of program termination have sued under Title IX claiming that the fundamental purpose of Title IX was not to eliminate men's programs and such termination amounts to a form of reverse discrimination. However, such claims appear to have no merit under most judicial decisions.

In 1993, the men's swimming team at the University of Illinois was cut while the women's was not. The men's

---

[41] *Id* at pp. 114-115

fencing team and both diving teams were eliminated as well. As usual, cutbacks were announced due to financial reasons. Members of the men's team sued, claiming discrimination on the basis of sex. Both the trial court and court of appeals held that such decision making by the University of Illinois was acceptable under Title IX analysis, particularly since the men's participation in athletics was 76.6 percent while the overall male enrollment was 56 percent.[42]

Title IX does not require schools to cut men's teams. College administrators make that choice rather than raise additional funding to support men and women's programs on an equal footing.

**Women Competing on Male Teams**

According to the guidelines issued by the OCR, if a college has a men's team but no women's team in a given sport, female athletes must be allowed to try out for the team unless it is a contact sport. As stated earlier, Duke University allowed Heather Sue Mercer to try out for the football team as a placekicker. Mercer was listed on the spring roster but was not allowed to attend a summer training camp or dress for the games. She was later cut from the team, and she sued Duke University alleging that once she was allowed on the team, Duke has discriminated against her by treating her less favorable than men. In October 2000, a federal jury ordered Duke to pay $1 in actual damages and $2 million in punitive damages.

**Men Competing on Women's Teams**

Some men attempt to compete on women's teams,

---

[42] *Id* at p. 115

especially when a comparable male sport is not offered by the college or university. Such exclusions, however, are usually upheld by the courts under the view that Title IX was meant to help the historically underrepresented sex. Still, one recent case may provide hope for those males desiring to try out for women's teams. In *Williams v. School Dist. of Bethlehem,* 799 F. Supp. 513 (E.D. Pa. 1992), the court ruled that a boy could compete on a woman's field hockey team because otherwise his equal protection rights would be violated.[43]

**Equity in Athletics Disclosure Act,** 20 U.S.C. 1092(g) -- 34 CFR 668.48.

The Equity in Athletics Disclosure Act (EADA) requires co-educational colleges and universities that receive federal funds and maintain an intercollegiate athletic program to prepare an annual report to the Department of Education. This report deals with such areas as athletic participation, staffing, revenues and expenses, by men's and women's teams. This act was first adopted in 1994 to provide Congress and the public with a snapshot of collegiate athletics participation by gender. The Department of Education uses this information in preparing its required report to Congress on gender equity in intercollegiate athletics. Such reports provide a valuable tool for assessing compliance with Title IX. Each university must compete numerous forms that provide public access to certain items.

Federal regulations require that the information, based on the previous reporting year, be made available for inspection by students, prospective students, and the public by October 30 of each year. A table must be completed that lists sports participants (including walk-

---

[43] *Sports Law* at p. 116 by Adam Epstein, Delmar Leaning (2003)

ons), operating expenses for men's and women's programs, recruiting expenses, scholarships awarded, revenues, and all coaches salaries. Once the data is received by the Department of Education, it must provide a report to Congress on gender trends in intercollegiate athletics based on these reports and make institutional specific reports available to the public through the Internet.[44]

**Equal Pay Act of 1963,** 29 U.S.C.A. § 206(b)

Women coaches, trainers, and administrators have increasingly sued colleges and universities for gender discrimination under the Equal Pay Act (EPA). This act requires virtually all employers to provide equal pay for men and women performing similar work. If a female employee sues under the EPA, she must prove that her employer paid her less than a male for substantially equal work. Crucial to this analysis, however, is that exceptions are made for differences in pay based upon an established seniority system, a merit system, a system that measures earnings by quantity or quality of production, or any other differential based upon a legitimate factor.

---

[44] *Id* at p. 117

# IX.   DRUGS AND TESTING

Drug use by athletes has been a controversial issue for many years. Athletes often use artificial stimulants to give them a physical and mental advantage over their opponents. The use of performance- enhancing drugs can be traced to the ancient Olympic Games where fame and fortune were rewarded, just as today, for athletic success. Drug testing of athletes is becoming common in all sports to one degree or the other. This raises constitutional issues including the right to privacy and due process protections from illegal searches and seizures, particularly since testing involves an analysis of a sample from urine or blood. Performance-enhancing drugs are substances athletes inject or consume to increase the human body's ability to perform during training sessions and sports contests. This includes common, over-the-counter muscle-building supplements, recovery products, and endurance-enhancing blood doping. Performance-enhancing drugs might be consumed orally or via needle injection.

When the government or a governmental entity such as a public school or public college desires to test a student-athlete for drugs, this constitutes state action. There is no state action for private sports leagues, and therefore the fourth, fifth, and fourteenth Amendment issues are generally not applicable in such context unless such testing is established by contract. Federal laws that regulate drug use and distribution include the Anabolic

Steroid Control Act of 1990. Steroids are artificial and synthetic forms of hormones, such as testosterone, that improve muscle building, growth, and repair. Since the government (state) desires to invade the privacy of athletes by testing their urine or blood for drugs, athletes have constitutional safeguards that allow a challenge to such a test on the grounds of its constitutionality. Numerous challenges to such policies have failed, and recently courts have given support to the use of mandatory, suspicion- less testing. Still, private organizations have their own testing policies that usually require consent to such policies (including appeals) as a condition for participating in that league.[45]

**Fourth Amendment**

Any time a *governmental agency* tests an athlete for drugs, it must comply with the Fourth Amendment, which states:

*The right of the people to be secure in their persons, houses, papers and effects against unreasonable searches and seizures, shall not be violated and no Warrants shall issue, but upon probable cause, supported by Oath or affirmation and particularly describing the place to be searched and the persons things to be seized.*

While many athletes now understand that being tested is a necessary part of the nature of competition, numerous cases have reached the courts to determine whether or not an individual athlete has a legitimate *expectation of privacy* when it comes to drug testing.[46]

In a decision involving Oklahoma high school's drug testing policy, the U.S. Supreme Court held in *Vernonia*

---

[45] *Sports Law* at p. 164 by Adam Epstein, Delmar Leaning (2003)
[46] *Id*

*School District v. Acton,* 515 U.S. 646 (1995) that high school athletes have a lower expectation of privacy than the public in general, and that mandating testing policies nationwide are valid as a condition for participating in high school sports. Additionally, though there may not be probable cause *per se* in testing high school athletes, the Supreme Court affirmed that public school districts do have special needs. The Court held that random drug testing was valid since such programs serve a compelling interest in public systems to deter the use of drugs.

## Fifth Amendment

Another constitutional consideration for drug testing of athletes is the Fifth Amendment, which provides:

*No person shall be deprived of life, liberty, or property, without due process of law; nor shall private property be taken for public use, without just compensation.*

An athlete should be granted a process for a hearing and appealing a positive drug test result. The right to go to school or participate in athletics is a property right.[47]

## NCAA Regulation

Intercollegiate athletes must sign a consent form in order to play college sports under the National Collegiate Athletic Association's policies. The NCAA established its own drug testing program in 1986 and comprehensively tests for both illegal street drugs and performance-enhancing drugs. Whether the NCAA is a *state actor*[48] is

---

[47] *Id* at p. 165

[48] The term *state actor* is used in United States civil rights law to describe a person who is acting on behalf of a governmental body, and is therefore subject to regulation under the United States bill of rights including the Fourth and Fifth Amendments, which prohibit the federal and state governments from violating certain rights and freedoms

subject to debate, though the answer seems to be that it is not and therefore is characterized as a private actor.[49]

**Professional Sports**

Major professional sports in the United States coordinate their own drug testing and use policies through collective bargaining agreements (CBAs) or consent from the professional athletes from their individual professional contract. The major aim of professional sports and drug testing appears to be treatment for the offender rather than punishment. Such a policy is much different than the Olympic Games where punishment and future deterrence appears to be the primary concern. [50]

One of the major concerns with drug testing in professional sports is that there is no uniform standard that applies to the NFL, NBA, NHL, and MLB. Each has different testing for a variety of drugs and punishments and treatment are different in each league. Additionally, there is confusion as to what drugs should be banned since the spectators themselves could legally purchase certain performance-enhancing training supplements at the local supermarket while the athletes could be punished for using the same supplements. Drug testing issues in professional sports center on contract and consent issues rather than constitutional issues.[51]

**National Football League**

The National Football League prohibits the illegal use of drugs and the abuse of prescription drugs, over-the-counter drugs, and alcohol. This applies to all players who

---

[49] *Sports Law* at p. 179 by Adam Epstein, Delmar Leaning (2003)
[50] *Id* p. 179
[51] *Id.* at pp. 179-180

have not yet retired from the league. However, the NFL's collective bargaining agreement sets the sole and exclusive means of testing for drugs and treating those players who have positive results. The National Football League's program is called the Intervention Program and purportedly establishes the appropriate levels of discipline. However, NFL players are only tested for cocaine, marijuana, amphetamines, morphine, codeine, and PCP. All players are tested in April and August, during the preseason.[52]

## The Olympic Games

The International Olympic Committee (IOC) has taken a more proactive stance on the prevention of the use of performance-enhancing drugs than any other organization in the world. In 1968 the IOC established the first testing of 40 International Olympic Committee athletes in Grenoble, France's Winter Olympic Games. One of the more famous cases involving an Olympic athlete was the use of illegal steroids by Canadian track star Ben Johnson in 1988 during the Seoul, Korea, Games. The Olympic Movement has set the standard for both competition drug testing and out of competition testing. However, enforcement is often the sole responsibility of each country's national Olympic committee (NOC) and the particular national governing body (NGB) for that particular Olympic sport.[53]

## International Olympic Committee Policies

*While many top U.S. Olympic caliber athletes have been drug tested throughout their careers, few have truly understood the drug testing process. The ever-changing*

---

[52] *Id.* at p. 180
[53] *Id.*

*rules and regulations, as well as the increase in number of doping control programs, while appearing to assist in the fight against doping in sport, have proven to be confusing and sometimes inconsistent. Many organizations cannot interpret their own rules, nor do they fully understand the jurisdictional issues that arise with respect to every sample taken until they are caught in a crisis.*[54]

The collection process of drug testing includes dividing a urine sample into two (2) containers, respectively known as the "A" sample and the "B" sample. The "A" sample is always analyzed first. The "B" sample is only analyzed in the event the "A" sample reveals the presence of a prohibited substance.

Drug testing of athletes is becoming common in all sports to one degree or the other. This raises constitutional issues including the right to privacy and due process protections from illegal searches and seizures, particularly since testing involves an analysis of a sample from urine or blood. Performance-enhancing drugs are substances athletes inject or consume to increase the human body's ability to perform during training sessions and sports contests. This includes common, over-the-counter muscle-building supplements, recovery products, and endurance-enhancing blood doping. Performance-enhancing drugs might be consumed orally or via needle injection.

Each sport within the Olympic Movement has a national federation, which is responsible for coordinating the activity for that particular sport in the country. In the United

---

[54] A Journey Through Olympic Drug Testing Rules: A Practitioner's Guide to Understanding Drug Testing Within the Olympic Movement, submitted by: Jill Pilgrim and Kim Betz, *The Sport Journal*, United States Sports Academy, http://www.thesportjournal.org/article/journey-through-olympic-drug-testing-rules-practitioners-guide-understanding-drug-testing-wi

States these federations are known as national governing bodies (NGB). The USOC has set forth a "due process" checklist and each NGB is required to comply with this list. It includes:

- notice of the specific charges,

- *reasonable* time between the receipt of notice of charges and the hearing,

- the right to have the hearing conducted at a convenient time and place,

- the right to be assisted in the presentation of one's case at the hearing before a disinterested and impartial body of fact finders,

- the right to call witnesses and present both written and oral evidence,

- the right to cross-examine, the right to a record of the hearing,

- the right to a written decision, and

- the right to written notice of appeal procedures.[55]

When the government or a governmental entity such as a public school or public college desires to test a student-athlete for drugs, this constitutes *state action*. There is no state action for private sports leagues, and therefore the Fourth, Fifth, and Fourteenth Amendment issues are generally not applicable in such context unless such testing is established by contract. Federal laws that regulate drug use and distribution include the Anabolic Steroid Control Act of 1990. Steroids are artificial and synthetic forms of hormones, such as testosterone, that

---

[55] Id

improve muscle building, growth, and repair. Since the government (state) desires to invade the privacy of athletes by testing their urine or blood for drugs, athletes have constitutional safeguards that allow a challenge to such a test on the grounds of its constitutionality. Numerous challenges to such policies have failed, and recently courts have given support to the use of mandatory, suspicion- less testing. Still, private organizations have their own testing policies that usually require consent to such policies (including appeals) as a condition for participating in that league.

## Consent Form by College or University Student Athlete to Drug Testing

http://www.uslegalforms.com/us/US-00956BG.htm

# X.   INTERNATIONAL SPORTS ISSUES

International sports issues and the law revolve primarily around the Olympic Games. The international Olympic rules, policies, and procedures have faced national and international legal challenges and other disputes including outright boycotts since it began again back in 1896. As exposure of the Olympics has increased, so too has the money involved in the Olympic Games at all levels. Athletes compete for international fame and fortune by winning a medal.[56]

Professional athletes are now commonplace during the Olympics as well. In fact, the United States sent professional basketball players such as Michael Jordan to compete in the summer games in Barcelona, Spain, in 1992. The U.S. Olympic Committee now awards cash prizes to American athletes based on their performance at the Olympics, a practice that other countries have offered for a long time.

**Competition for and During the Olympic Games**

Countries, as well as states and provinces within countries, fiercely compete for the ability to hold the Olympic Games within their borders. The possibility of sizeable monetary rewards to athletes has tempted many Olympic participants to use illegal and unethical means to obtain an unfair advantage over other competitors despite the Olympic system's set of strict guidelines and rules with regard to

---

[56] *Id.* pp.191

illegal drugs. Additionally, the IOC has suspended and permanently banned many medal competitors (and sometimes winners) for violations of the rules.[57]

## The Olympic Movement

The modern Olympic Games began in 1896 in Athens, Greece. At that time, athletes were thought to compete in the Olympic Games in an international setting only as amateurs. In other words, a competitor was seen as someone who competed only for the love of the sport without regard to financial rewards or fame. Today, the Olympics are no longer just for amateurs. Professional athletes are also allowed to compete.

Unfortunately, the Olympic Games have become increasingly commercialized and now serve as a showcase for major countries, athletes, corporate promotions and international politics. While the Olympic Games are supposed to unite the world through sport, international politics have interfered. At the1936 Berlin Olympics, Adolf Hitler refused to recognize African American Jesse Owens' four gold medals, a wonder at that time The 1992 Munich (West Germany) Games were marred by tragedy when Arab terrorists killed Israeli athletes and took nine other hostages.

During the 1976 Montreal Olympics Games, the Canadian governments refused to allow Taiwan's team to carry its flag or have its national anthem played at the games. Also, in Montreal, several African nations demanded that New Zealand be prevented from competing because one of its rugby teams had played in South Africa, at that time a racially segregationist nation. Thirty-one nations withdrew

---

[57] *Id.* pp.192

their teams from the 1976 Olympics competition as a result of New Zealand's refusal. The United States boycotted the 1980 Moscow Olympics to protest the Soviet Union's invasion of Afghanistan. More than 60 other nations boycotted this event as well. As a result, the Soviet Union and 15 other nations withdrew from the 1984 Games in Los Angeles.[58]

The 1992 Olympics in Barcelona, Spain, included the Unified Team (with athletes from 12 former Soviet republics), a reunited Germany, and South Africa, appearing for the first time since 1960. At the 2000 Olympics in Sydney, Australia, North and South Korea entered the games under one flag, although they competed as separate countries.[59]

The *Olympic Movement* is the general term used to describe the International Olympic system of rules, regulations, policies, and procedures. The International Olympic Committee (IOC) was established in 1894 for the 1896 Olympics in Athens, Greece. The IOC's headquarters are in Lausanne, Switzerland. It sets and enforces Olympic policies. As of 2000, the IOC recognized 199 national Olympic committees, including the U.S. Olympic Committee. The USOC is currently headquartered in Colorado Springs, Colorado. The IOC normally chooses the site of future games at least six years in advance.[60] The IOC is a very powerful body. It cannot force its rules on national governments, but countries that wish to participate in the Olympics must agree to its procedures.

Every person or organization that plays any part

---

[58] *Id.* p.193
[59] *Id.*
[60] *Id.* p.194

whatsoever in the Olympic Movement has to accept the supreme authority of the IOC and be bound by its Rules and submit to its jurisdiction. It is the supreme authority in decisions regarding the suspension, expulsion, or disqualification of all athletes.[61] Being the supreme authority of the Olympic Movement, the IOC is the final authority on all questions concerning the Olympic Games and the Olympic Movement, including matters of discipline affecting athletes and coaches. Additionally, the IOC is the final arbiter for permanent and temporary penalties of all kinds, the heaviest of which are suspension, expulsion, disqualification, and exclusion. The powers of the IOC are absolute. It delegates to the International Federations (IFs), however, the technical control of the sports they govern. The IOC has recently emphasized that decisions involving its own rules must be submitted to binding arbitration under the Court of Arbitration for Sport. [62]

The IOC relies heavily on the International Federations governing individual sports to enforce its rules and regulations. The IOC delegates to individual IF's the technical control of all aspects of the sport they supervise as well as authority for suspending or disciplining individual who violate the IF's rules or codes of conduct. However, sometimes domestic (national) rights of the individual athletes conflict with the rules of the IOC or the IFs. Additionally, it is possible that athletes from one country might be treated differently from athletes from another country. This has led to numerous domestic and international lawsuits. The introduction of the International Council of Arbitration for Sport (ICAS) and its supervision over the CAS were designed to deal with ensuring that

---

[61] *Id.*
[62] *Id.*

athletes around the world are treated the same for similar violations of the Olympic Movement.[63]

The IOC recognizes national Olympic committees (NOCs) as the sole authorities responsible for representing their respective countries at the Olympic Games as well as at other events sponsored by the IOC. For the United States, the NOC is the United States Olympic Committee (USOC), which was originally chartered by Congress as an independent corporation on September 21, 1950. The USOC exercises exclusive jurisdiction over all matters pertaining to the participation of the United States in the Olympic Games and in the Pan American Games. As stated in an earlier chapter, each sport within the Olympic Movement has a national federation, which is responsible for coordinating the activity for that particular sport in the country. In the United States these federations are known as national governing bodies (NGB).

The USOC is charged with providing resolution of conflicts and disputes involving amateur athletes, national governing bodies, and amateur sports organizations and with protecting the opportunity of any amateur athlete to participate in amateur athletic competition. Swift resolution of legal disputes, however, has not always been possible.[64]

The authority for the creation of National Governing Bodies is found in the Amateur Sports Act. The authority of the NGBs includes recommending individual athletes to the USOC for participation in the Olympic or Pan American Games as well as establishing internal procedures for determining eligibility standards. The NGBs are responsible both to the USOC (and U.S. courts) and to the

---

[63] *Id.* pp.195
[64] *Id.*

IF for their sport. In an eligibility dispute, the first decision to suspend a U.S. athlete most likely to come from an NGB, but the IF may declare the athlete ineligible without a prior action by an NGB. This has led to vicious legal battles. However, the addition of the CAS has helped in resolving these disputes more quickly. [65]

The Ted Stevens Olympic and Amateur Sports Act established the United States Olympic Committee and provided for the national governing bodies for each Olympic sport. The Act provides important legal protection for individual athletes.[66]

Prior to the adoption of the Act in 1978, the Amateur Athletic Union (AAU) represented the United States on international competition matters and regulated amateur sports generally. The AAU had adopted arbitrary rules which prohibited women from participating in running events and banned any runner who had raced in the same event as a runner with a shoe-company sponsorship. In response to criticisms of the AAU, Congress adopted the Act, effectively removing that organization from any governance role. The AAU now continues as a voluntary organization largely promoting youth track.

The Amateur Sports Act charters the US Olympic Committee, which in turn can charter a national governing body (NGB) for each sport, such as USA Swimming, the United States Ski Team or the United States Figure Skating Association. Each NGB in turn establishes the rules for selecting the United States Olympic Team and promotes amateur competition in that sport. The Act requires that active athletes (defined as amateur athletes

---

[65] *Id.*
[66] *Id.* pp.198

who have represented the United States in international amateur competition within the last ten years) must hold 20 percent of the voting power of any board or committee in an NGB. The Act also provides athletes with due process and appeal rights concerning eligibility disputes.[67]

The Act gives exclusive rights of usage of the words *Olympic* and *Olympiad* to the Olympic Committee. The Committee used this act to sue other organizations which used this term "Olympics", such as the Gay Olympics.[68]

The United States government controls the very existence of the USOC. In seeking protection from suspension procedures, many athletes have attempted to obtain shelter in the due process provision of the Fifth Amendment to the U.S. Constitution but have failed each time.[69] The United States Olympic Committee and now the United States Anti-Doping Agency, both serve as "private" regulators for the United States Olympic Movement. This private sector status of sport regulation in the United States has created a significant accountability vacuum. As a result, athletes' constitutional liberty and property interests are threatened because athletes are not given meaningful due process protections to protect their eligibility. Steps should be taken to promote greater accountability for the United States Olympic Movement, so that the athletes who serve to enhance our nation's prestige do not risk their due process rights in the process.[70]

---

[67] Id.

[68] Id.

[69] Id.

[70] Dionne L. Koller, *How the United States Government Sacrifices Athletes' Constitutional Rights in the Pursuit of National Prestige.* B.Y.U. Law Rev., Fall 2008.

www.ingramcontent.com/pod-product-compliance
Lightning Source LLC
Chambersburg PA
CBHW031943190326
41519CB00007B/631